AN EARLY CHILDHOOD CURRICULUM FOR MULTIPLY HANDICAPPED CHILDREN

AN EARLY CHILDHOOD CURRICULUM FOR MULTIPLY HANDICAPPED CHILDREN

Regina Schattner

The John Day Company   New York

The John Day Company, 257 Park Avenue South, New York N. Y. 10010

an **Intext** publisher

Published on the same day in Canada by Longman Canada Limited.

Library of Congress Catalogue Card Number: 72-132948
Printed in the United States of America

Dedicated with love and gratitude for
all the joy they have given me

To Heather, Scott,
and Daniel

Foreword

Early education for exceptional children and education for the multiply handicapped are the leading priorities in special education on national, state, and local levels. Regina Schattner, through her fifteen years of working with young multiply handicapped children, is uniquely qualified and experienced in both of these areas. In this landmark book she has contributed new insights into the problems of defining and dealing with the multiply handicapped.

She defines the multiply handicapped child as one "with a number of deficits which result in special problems of learning and growth." These deficits stem from impairment in the intellectual, sensorimotor, and affective domains of human abilities.

Very little is known about the impact of multiple defects on a person's physical, emotional, social, and mental growth and development. For a long time special educators have been "locked into" various disability compartments. Useful as these compartments have been, they have begun to be more of a deterrent than a facilitator in special education, particularly when applied to the multiply handicapped child. It can be hypothesized that problems faced by this child cannot be measured merely by the effect of each of his handicaps separately, but, rather, must be considered synergetically. By the same token, a teacher of the multiply handicapped who studies only separate special educational interventions for the blind, for the deaf, for the mentally retarded, for the emotionally disturbed, for the crippled, or for the neurologically impaired cannot be expected to be adequately prepared to plan and develop a meaningful educational program.

With this in mind, the author has prepared a guide for understanding the multidimensional educational problems of the multiply handicapped child, as well as for developing an appropriate curriculum in an appropriate setting.

It is hoped that this pioneering volume will stimulate other practitioners in the field to report their experiences, enthusiasm, insights, and experimentations.

I. Ignacy Goldberg
Professor of Education
Department of Special Education
Teachers College, Columbia University

CONTENTS

Introduction

This book is the result of fifteen years of experience working with young multiply handicapped children.

I hope it will be used as a resource by teachers: that is the intent with which it was written. During my years as a teacher and a director of programs for multiply handicapped children, I have found that the greatest asset to special education is the classroom teacher. But so often the teacher has to act as a pioneer. Too often, unfortunately, she works in isolation from other teachers who are grappling with the same problems in educating special children. Each teacher makes a new beginning and discovers new methods and materials for working with multiply handicapped children. The curriculum presented in this book is an abstraction of the experiences of many teachers working with multiply handicapped.

The program is based on the principles of early childhood development. It is developed within a framework of exploring and interpreting the environment. A living, creative curriculum, it makes special use of play, music, arts and crafts, dramatics, and an enriched language program to serve some of the special needs of multiply handicapped children who can function in a school setting. The purpose of the curriculum is to provide rich experiences to compensate for the deprivation of the early years and to prepare the children for their next phase of development.

The curriculum also offers methods and materials used in preparing multiply handicapped children for academic learning.

This special curriculum can be adapted for the child with motor and sensory deficits, with mental retardation, and with emotional disturbance. The multiply handicapped child, for whom this curriculum is in the main designed, is the child with a number of deficits which resulted in special problems of learning and growth. At the same time, he is a child with the same basic needs and drives as the nonhandicapped child.

*Keep in mind that it is our
basic philosophy to develop in every
human being his uppermost potential
creative ability regardless of the
degree of his handicap.*

—*Viktor Lowenfeld*

Chapter **1**

WHO IS THE MULTIPLY HANDICAPPED CHILD?

Discovery of the Multiply Handicapped Child

We are only now beginning to discover the multiply handicapped child; although he has been with us for a long time, we have not recognized his existence. We have been accustomed to think in terms of the blind child, the crippled child, the cerebral palsied child, the deaf child. As we learn more about these children, we discover that the child who is blind may have a hearing loss. A physically handicapped child may be mentally retarded also. A mentally retarded child may have epilepsy and a visual problem. Cerebral palsy in itself is a multiple handicap. Children may have more than two disabilities. While working with children who have been diagnosed as blind, deaf, and so on, we discover that they have other handicaps and learning disabilities.

Today we are beginning to identify children with multiple handicaps. The first steps are being taken to provide facilities for diagnosis, treatment, and referral. As Dr. Edward Davens has observed, "Two encouraging trends, which began well before the 1960 White House Conference, have continued in an accelerated pace in recent years: (1) the tendency for State crippled children's programs to broaden their definition of a handicapped child to include an increasing variety of conditions; and (2) a tendency to drop illogical and untenable restrictions from these programs, such as those preventing a physically handicapped child who also has mental retardation from receiving treatment."[1] Once we have found and identified this child, we are committed to his education.

Educational Identification of the Multiply Handicapped Child

The number of handicaps does not necessarily identify the multiply handicapped child who has need of a special program. A partially sighted child with a slight limp has more than one handicap, but he may be able to function quite well in a classroom with normal children. A child with cerebral palsy and epilepsy may have some involvement in his hands and a slight problem in articulation. His seizures may be controlled by medication. The degree to which his handicaps affect his functioning is so slight that this child may be integrated into a class for children with cerebral palsy.

In other children who have cerebral palsy, the neuromuscular involvement is so extensive that they cannot walk and their speech is practically impossible to understand. These children are multiply handicapped, although they have been diagnosed as having a single disability. Some children with one physical deficit may have severe behavior problems that call for a special program geared to the needs of the multiply handicapped child. The number and types of handicaps do not always determine the need for special placement.

Placement in a special program for the multiply handicapped should be based on the total functioning of the child. For example, a blind child with an orthopedic handicap is a multiply handicapped child. Blindness is a primary sensory loss. If in addition there is an orthopedic handicap, the child's whole development is affected. The orthopedic handicap will affect his ability to explore his environment, necessitating special use of auditory and tactual clues. The child will have a problem of locating himself in space. He will need the services of two specialists—one who can teach a blind child self-help and other skills, and a physical therapist who can help him develop motor skills.

But the need goes beyond a program that includes two specialists.

[1]Edward Davens, "A View of Health Services for Mothers and Children," *Children* 12 (March-April 1965):53.

The basic need is for a program in which the child is treated as a totality. The danger exists that the specialists will treat only the handicap. The child needs a program geared to his total development, whereas specialists work to remediate special learning problems. Specialists sometimes limit themselves or are limited to one area of disability. They treat the deficit, not the child. What is needed is a program based on the principles of early childhood development, allowing specialists to work with children within the framework of an all-inclusive program for childhood development. Special skills and expertise certainly can be brought into the program for the multiply handicapped, but it is the child who must be the center of the program.

Definition, referral, and placement are not administrative problems. Involved in the whole question of definition is a better understanding of the handicapped child and the provision of more adequate services to meet his needs. As stated by Dr. Davens: "During the next five years, there are likely to be further trends toward broadening the definition of handicapped children and toward the organization of services and facilities to permit an integrated approach to the whole child, regardless of the numbers, type, or combination of handicaps."[2]

Educational Needs of the Young Multiply Handicapped Child

In many ways special education has acted as a pioneer in the whole field of education. For a long time psychologists and teachers have recognized the need to bring a handicapped child into an educational setting at a very early stage in his life. According to Janet Pomeroy, "The downward extension of the legal chronological and mental age for admission to public educational programs is an absolute essential for a large percentage of our child population. In this spirit Colorado has established the lower limit for exceptional children at three years of age."[3]

There are, however, very few facilities for the young handicapped child: "Provision of special classes in public schools or

[2] *Ibid.*
[3] Janet Pomeroy, *Recreation for the Physically Handicapped* (New York: Macmillan Co., 1964), p. 7.

special day schools for the multiple handicapped is a relatively recent development; in many communities they have been established during the past ten or fifteen years,"[4] comment William Cruickshank and Orville Johnson.

One can anticipate that with the growing consciousness of the need to educate disadvantaged children at an early age there also will be more awareness of the need to bring handicapped children into the public educational system during the early years of childhood. We may very well see a growth of preschool centers for handicapped children. The whole field of education is in ferment. Special education is also undergoing changes. But until there is a further broadening of the definition of handicapped children and the provision of more preschool centers, the teachers of multiply handicapped children will be working with children with a wide range of ages, handicaps, and emotional and learning problems. Because of the lack of preschool centers for multiply handicapped children, many of them enter school when they are seven years of age or even older. Even though their chronological ages are well beyond early childhood, these children have missed many of the experiences and development of the early years. The school is the only agency that can help to remediate these gaps.

The Early Years of the Normal Child

From the time he is an infant, the normal child uses his body and his senses to explore his environment and to gain concepts about himself. When the baby crawls around the furniture and plays peek-a-boo with his mother, he learns about spatial orientation and control of his muscles. He finds out which furniture is hard or soft. He learns that he can not see through furniture and that someone may be present even when he can not see him. He learns that some things are mobile and others are stationary. He experiments constantly and he learns by doing. He watches his brothers and sisters and imitates them.

Every mother can remember how her child learned some "truths." I recall my own daughter playing on the floor and sud-

---

[4]William Cruickshank and Orville Johnson, *Education of Exceptional Children and Youth* (Englewood Cliffs, N.J.: Prentice-Hall, 1958), p. 97.

denly seeing a patch of sunlight. She crawled over and put out both hands to catch the sun. But when she opened her hands—no sun. The small child is constantly exploring and testing his environment. He uses all his senses to investigate the properties of objects. After a time he begins to learn single words to identify objects and people. By learning their names he begins to abstract objects from the background of his environment. He makes the first move toward self-identification.

Selma H. Fraiberg, discussing the process of growth for the normal child, stated: "The world he discovers is a vast and intricate jig-saw puzzle, thousands of pieces scrambled together in a crazy juxtaposition. Piece by piece he assembles the fragments into whole objects, objects into groups, until he emerges with a fairly coherent picture of the tiny piece of world he inhabits . . . He is intoxicated with his newfound world; he devours it with every sense organ."[5]

The young child is full of boundless energy. He runs and hops and skips and jumps. With his whole body he enjoys the sensations of moving through space and glories in each newly acquired skill. Through experience he learns to cope with his environment. He is no longer completely powerless and dependent on adults.

During the first three years of life, the child's command of words grows at a precipitate rate. According to Kornie Chukovsky, "At the age of about one year the child knows less than ten words; at the end of two years his vocabulary has grown to 250 or 300 words and by the end of his third year it is in the thousands."[6] He uses language not only to structure his world and to gain knowledge, but also as a means of communication.

During these years the child learns to be independent in the activities of daily living—toileting, washing, dressing, and feeding. He makes the distinction between *I* and *you* and begins to build his self-image. Slowly he breaks away from complete dependence on his family and moves toward relationships with other children.

By the time he enters school, the child has developed from a helpless infant, utterly dependent on adults for the satisfaction of all his needs, to a child who has achieved a measure of mastery of

---

[5]Selma H. Fraiberg, *The Magic Years* (New York: Scribner's Sons, 1959), p. 54.
[6]Kornie Chukovsky, *From Two to Five* (Berkeley: University of California Press, 1963), p. 10.

his own body, a facility with language, skills in the activities of daily living, a concept of himself and his environment, and the beginning of independence from his family. He has acquired the rudiments of social behavior and self-discipline.

This young child has been through a series of profound emotional experiences common to the developmental process of all normal children. His level of awareness and activity is the result of six years of enormous change and growth.

Every child does not achieve this optimum development in all areas, but every normal child does have the potential for it. For the handicapped child this kind of maturation is impossible.

The Early Years of the Multiply Handicapped Child

The early years of a multiply handicapped child are very different from those of the normal child. The intent here is not to compare normal with handicapped children, but rather to highlight the nature of the deprivation of the handicapped child's early years and the consequent effect on his growth—his knowledge of the environment, his concept of himself, and his relations with others.

From birth the multiply handicapped child is deprived. Because of sensory motor losses he cannot run about freely to explore and investigate his environment. His sensory losses result in decreased stimulation from the external world. As a result the brain itself is understimulated. Paul V. Lemkau has explained this effect:

The brain is put together so that it can integrate and make meaningful the information brought in through the senses. Normally, this inflow of sensory input is in a certain balance each sense with the other. We do not know today exactly what this balance is nor can we make quantitative measurements of how much sight and how much hearing and how much taste and smell or balance and position sense enter the normal inflow, but we do know that the normal brain is equipped to handle it and make it meaningful . . .

Suppose now that this balanced inflow is interfered with by decreased sight or hearing. This represents a loss of stimulation, a deprivation of experience to the individual concerned. That part of his brain used to "integrate" the material from these senses would also be understimulated.[7]

The young multiply handicapped child has a very poor self-image. He has been deprived of almost all of the early childhood experiences that help to develop a strong sense of self. His concept of his environment is fragmentary and distorted. He remains dependent on his mother for a much longer period of time than the normal child.

Because of the multiple nature of their handicaps these children may spend a great deal of time in clinics and hospitals. It is not unusual for them to undergo surgery at an early age. This requires a long period of separation from the family and then a period of anxiety before the effects of the surgery are known. When it is necessary to hospitalize a child for a "thorough work-up," there is also a painful separation from home and family and the necessity of coping with a new and frightening environment. For most of the child's early years, the family concentrates on trying to find some means to remedy his physical handicaps. During the course of these early formative years the child is exposed to many adults who are concerned mainly with his physical functioning.

The young handicapped child presents a picture of incomplete and uneven development. For example, a child with severe motor disability may have the physical competence of an infant and yet may be able to use language for communicating and for gaining knowledge of his environment. Another child may have good motor skills and be fairly independent in all the activities of daily living, but because of a speech handicap and a visual problem he may communicate largely through gestures and rely on tactual and auditory clues to orient himself to his environment.

Among such children there are likely to be extreme differences in behavior. Each child reflects the effects of his handicaps, his early experiences, and the attitudes of adults who have worked with him. Children whose parents raise them in a warm, accepting atmosphere and guide their growth toward emotional maturity may be

[7]Paul V. Lemkau, "The Influence of Handicapping Conditions on Child Development," *Children* 8 (March-April 1961):45.

outgoing, cheerful, and able to relate easily to other children and adults. Other children may be very withdrawn, some very demanding. There are children in this category who talk constantly, whether or not anyone is listening. Others very rarely speak, and often not unless they are directly addressed. Some may have a vocabulary limited to single words, and some children make no use at all of language.

Extremely demonstrative children may bestow affection with little discrimination; their emotions lack tone and feeling. Some children may climb all over an adult, while others may be aloof and draw back from any physical contact.

Multiply handicapped children have motor, sensory, and intellectual losses, but even beyond the "crippling" effects of these multiple handicaps there is a deficit in the total personality development. This "damage" varies from child to child. One cannot categorize these children; they do not fit neatly into pigeon holes. How would one define the child with an I.Q. of 80, who is hyperactive, aggressive, partially sighted, and hard of hearing?

The teacher needs to know each child well in order to build an effective program. A great deal of her knowledge is gained from observation. To help interpret her observations she should discuss the child's behavior and competence with the psychologist and therapists who make up the school team. It should also be borne in mind that these children change. What appears to be a strong asset in the first year at school may help a child achieve a level of competence that may change his whole pattern of education.

In structuring a program for the young, multiply handicapped child, the teacher should understand the social behavior of the child. The term *social* covers all aspects of the child's personality development—how he feels about himself, how he relates to others, and how he accepts adults. In learning to know the child, the teacher may receive some help from records of his history, particularly from a psychological evaluation, but she will have to see the child in the school setting before she realistically can structure a program that will meet his social needs.

It will help a teacher if she understands some of the basis for the behavior of the multiply handicapped child in her classroom. The manifestations of the personality damage are different with each child. For example, a teacher should know that a mentally retarded child who has motor sensory deficits and who is difficult to reach, must have some emotional disturbance. The degree of disturbance will vary, but all multiply handicapped children suffer from some psychological damage.

In our society, which is so oriented toward norms of success and conformity, the multiply handicapped child differs in many social respects from the normal child. In our child oriented culture, the multiply handicapped child also presents a problem to his parents. While even a normal child needs support to grow up, the handicapped child needs special support not only from his parents but from society. In our society he is often denied this support, and accordingly he suffers from feelings of inadequacy, frustration, hostility, and anger.

The variations of personality problems are endless. Each individual child develops according to his own special pattern of growth. However, all multiply handicapped children have two things in common. First, each child's development is uneven in terms of his physical, sensory, mental, and emotional growth. Second, each child's over-all development is slower than that of the normal child, because the deficits affect his total growth.

Multiply handicapped children have strengths as well as weaknesses. With guidance and encouragement, many learn to walk with braces and crutches. They exert great strength to learn how to hold a pair of scissors. With smiles and good cheer, they will repay a teacher for many hours of hard work. When one thinks of all the deprivations of the early childhood years and the traumatic nature of many of their experiences, one can only marvel that multiply handicapped children develop as well as they do.

Early Childhood Experiences of Multiply Handicapped Children

In the early years of life, the multiply handicapped child and his family are beset with problems which affect the lives of all of them. Hopefully early diagnosis, referral, and placement in a special facility will alleviate some of the grief and bewilderment for the parents and result in rich early experiences for the child.

Described below are two examples of the way in which the early years of two multiply handicapped children were spent:

Frank was the first child of a fairly well-to-do family. His mother's pregnancy was uneventful, and Frank was a full-term baby. It was the grandmother who realized that something was wrong. The child did not sit, crawl, or pull himself to a standing position the way her own children had. He did not follow his mother with his eyes.

The family began the round of hospitals and agencies. They went to Columbia Presbyterian Medical Center, the New York Commission for the Blind, the Shield of David, the Lavalle School, Jacobi Hospital. In addition, the boy had a private physician and an ophthalmologist. Frank was diagnosed as mentally retarded, partially sighted due to optic atrophy, epileptic, and suffering from a mild form of cerebral palsy.

There was no facility for a young multiply handicapped child. Finally at seven and a half, he was placed in a special class at a public school. He had an I.Q. of 79; he made good use of language and had enough vision to see functionally. However, by the time he entered school, he had developed behavior problems which made it difficult to contain him in a class. He lasted only two weeks. Although he had been toilet trained before entering the school, he was so disturbed by the new experience that he lost all control. He had two accidents and was immediately suspended. It took his parents over a year to find a private school that was willing to take Frank on a trial basis.

Mimi had cerebral palsy. She was mentally retarded and autistic. She was known to the Association for the Help of Retarded Children, United Cerebral Palsy, Hospital for Special Surgery, New York Service for Orthopedically Handicapped. Her parents took her from one agency to another. She had psychological and physical work-ups. She was examined and evaluated. She was given physical therapy in an out-patient clinic, and her mother was given a regimen of exercises for Mimi to do at home.

For the first six years of her life, family and specialists concentrated entirely on Mimi's motor functioning. When she finally was accepted into a private school she was seven years of age.

She walked with crutches and wore long leg braces. She had sufficient vision to go from the bus to the school and to make her way around the school. She used single words to make her needs known, and had fairly good self-help skills. But her entire development had been in the motor area and self-help areas. She made no effort to reach out to other people, or to investigate her environment. She had no interest in objects or people; she was attracted only on occasion by a play of light. For the most part Mimi stood in the standing table and rocked back and forth.

Every teacher of multiply handicapped children will recognize Frank and Mimi. These are "their" children.

These are the children for whom the methods and materials in this book are designed. These are the children for whom the schools must create the early childhood experiences that are the birthright of all children.

Conclusion

A multiply handicapped child does not fit into any one category. The teacher has to see her children as developing human beings, not merely as cerebral palsied children, blind children, mentally retarded children, or brain injured children. What she sees are *children* with handicaps. The teacher has the opportunity to create a highly individualized program based on the needs that all children have for certain developmental experiences and on the knowledge that handicapped children have been deprived of those experiences.

An early childhood curriculum for multiply handicapped children should, therefore, include:

(1) Opportunities to explore and interpret the environment, based on an understanding of the children's lack of sensory stimulation and poor experiential background.

(2) An intensified physical education program, based on an understanding of the need for these children to develop gross and fine motor skills.

(3) A structured program of play, giving them opportunities to socialize with other children, based on the recognition that these children largely have lived in isolated, narrow environments with little chance to communicate with other children.

(4) Creative activities, based on the realization that these children, who are alienated from their environment, have poor self-images and a fragmented concept of their environment.

(5) An enriched language program, based on the recognition of the decisive role played by language in the whole process of learning and growth.

Chapter **2**

THE PHYSICAL PLANT

In a well-rounded program, the children will not be contained solely in one room. They should have access to a gym, where they can make use of special apparatus. And from the outset the teacher should view the outdoors as part of her classroom. But the children need to feel, too, that they belong. For the first year it is best to view the classroom as the home of this special group of children. Most activities should be conducted in it. The classroom is the environment wherein the teacher seeks to help build a community of children.

The Special Education Classroom

This room should be large, sunny, and painted in pastel colors. If possible, the floor should be covered with indoor-outdoor carpeting in a neutral shade. Walls and floors should provide a background effect that is restful and pleasing to the eye, but not stimulating. A rug gives the room a more inviting aspect. The room should be well lighted in all areas. With this kind of room as a background, the teacher can enrich the environment.

Wherever possible, the classroom should be on the ground floor, directly accessible to the street. The children are usually brought to school by bus, and have to walk or be brought from the bus to the classroom. If a classroom is situated on a higher floor, the children must have access to an elevator. Some multiply handicapped can not walk. Some walk with crutches, and for some of the children even an elevator may be a frightening experience. From many points of view, the classroom on the ground floor is best. It also makes it easier for the teacher to take the children outdoors for recreation and nature walks. The physical management of the children should be made as simple as possible.

If someone has to help children off a bus and then crowd them into an elevator—wheelchairs, crutches and all—the whole business of getting the children into the classroom becomes very complicated and time-consuming, demanding a great deal of organization.

Toilets

Toilets should be located as close to the classroom as possible. If, every time a child has to go to the toilet, the teacher has to arrange for someone to accompany him down a long hall, she will not be helping the child achieve independence in toileting.

One commode should be equipped with hand rails for children with poor balance. Each lavatory should have sinks low enough so that the children can turn on faucets independently, but the sinks should be of varying heights, since not all these children are physically small. Paper towel dispensers, too, should be low enough so that children can take towels by themselves. An early childhood curriculum for multiply handicapped children must emphasize teaching skills of daily living. Toileting and washing are important activities of daily living, in which the children have to achieve maximum independence.

The physical setup of the facility, therefore, has special importance for the multiply handicapped child. In planning the program this should be given the attention it merits.

Setting Up the Classroom

These children need a great variety of visual stimuli. They also need to learn about the environment through physical means—by moving through the environment either with help or independently. At this primitive level they do not learn through verbal teaching. First they have to be made sensorily aware of their environment.

The room should be set up so that there are different areas for different activities. One area should have motor equipment—climbing apparatus, a barrel to go through, a Bobo clown to punch, a small slide, etc. Another area should have tables and chairs for work. A third area should have large mats, on which children can roll or lie down to rest. The classroom should have cubicles where the children can hang their coats. Whenever possible, the classroom itself should have a sink, and near the sink should be the eating area.

A Multiple-Purpose Inner Room

If available, it is helpful to have a large closet fixed up so that a child can stay there by himself or work privately with a teacher. This large closet can have a half-door, high enough so that the child cannot climb out, and low enough so that he can be observed at all times. The floor may be carpeted. Furniture may include a rocker, a small table and a chair, some shelves, etc. Such a small, all-purpose room can be used to isolate a child who becomes very aggressive. It also can be used for a child who wants to listen to music by himself, by supplying a record player equipped with earphones. This room also can be used when the teacher wishes to work alone with one child, leaving her group in the care of an assistant. The teacher is still within call even while she gives one child individual attention. The room is also the "quiet room," free from distractions. Here a child may be alone when he feels the need.

In summary, then, the classroom for the multiply handicapped child should have a large gym area, a work area, an eating area equipped with a basin with running water, a rest area equipped with large mats, and a small, multiple-purpose room, which can be made out of a large closet. When there is not enough room, the work area and eating area can be the same.

It is best, however, for these children to learn by experience that some places and things are used for one purpose and others are used for different purposes. This is the most primitive means, through their own bodies, whereby they learn that there are differences.

Materials and Equipment

The appendix lists materials and equipment for the development of gross and fine motor skills, sensory development, perceptual development, and creative activities. In addition, the early childhood classroom for multiply handicapped children should include a standing table for the use of four children and a second standing table for the use of two children. These tables usually are used for physically handicapped children, but they can be used for hyperactive children also, as well as for children who need to be introduced to some form of parallel play. For physically handicapped children the standing table provides support. For hyperactive children the table provides a sense of security and restraint, and for disinterested children it provides the beginning of a group situation.

The tables can be ordered from any company that supplies orthopedic equipment to clinics and hospitals. Such a table has a Formica top, a slot in which the child stands, and a door which bolts on the outside. The child stands locked into his slot, and next to him stands another child. A timid child should be permitted to explore the table and be given every opportunity to get into and out of the slot himself. The table can help him come out of himself. The case of one very disturbed child illustrates this use. He would stand and watch the children in the table, go up to it, and then retreat. After a period of time he climbed into the table, then climbed right back out. After a few weeks he went into the slot, reached around in back, pulled the door, and bolted it. From that day on, that particular slot in the table belonged to him.

Another kind of special equipment which should be included is a supply of talking book machines with headphones which can be procured from the Library for the Blind in Washington, D.C. They have the great virtue of allowing a child to sit by himself, listening to music, while the rest of the group is engaged in other activities.

Visual Stimuli

The classroom of the multiply handicapped child should be full of visual clues. Each area should have pictures which indicate its utility. This will help a child to recognize function. In addition, mounted on a board should be a large photograph of each child, his name printed underneath. Smaller photographs of the children should be used on the cubicles.

The teacher has to think of bright colors and large forms that will attract the child's vision and prod him to go over and look at objects and decorations. The classroom must be rich in visual stimuli. Tables, chairs and cubicles should be labeled with various symbols and each child's name, not because he will learn to read, but because he may focus his vision and learn to associate a particular symbol and letters with himself. Although the visual stimuli should be rich, they also should be well organized so that the child is not bombarded. These stimuli also should be visual clues, which will help a child to understand his environment.

Summary

In her classroom the teacher creates the physical setting which may help motivate the child to explore, to reach out, to make contact with his environment. The room should be large, carefully organized for various activities, and decorated brightly with visual stimuli.

When the child enters this room it invites him to explore. It is *his* environment. There are pictures of himself, his classmates, and his teacher. He learns the function of each part of the room. Where he eats, there are large pictures of dishes and fruit. Where he works, there are pictures of children sitting at desks. In the gym area, he sees pictures of children climbing the jungle gym. It is a room full of children and the doings of children.

Chapter **3**

THE STAFF

The multiply handicapped child in school should be serviced by a team of professionals. The child may need speech therapy or physical therapy or both. Psychology contributes a great deal to understanding the behavior of multiply handicapped children. The teacher should be able to call on other specialists for help in both structuring and evaluating her program, but the focal person in the child's life at school is the teacher. She is the one who sees the child five times a week. He is with her throughout the day except for the periods he spends with the specialists. Therefore, the teacher must see the child as a total human being; she must build a unified program that integrates all professionals serving the child.

The home classroom staff should be composed of the teacher, her assistant, and an aide. The assistant, usually a paraprofessional or a teacher-in-training, can help prepare materials. She (or he) can work with one group of children under the teacher's guidance, while the teacher works with another group.

The aide can supervise the children in the lavatory. She can help take them outdoors. She can assist the children at lunch time, and help clean up after arts and crafts period.

The team of professionals may well include a pediatrician, a psychologist, an optometrist, a speech therapist, a physical therapist, a music teacher, a social worker, and a psychiatrist.

Multiply handicapped children need the services of a wide range of professionals with special skills. An educational program for multiply handicapped young children is really a program in how to help a "damaged" child achieve his childhood so that he can go on to develop and mature.

The Teacher

The teacher who implements the curriculum for the multiply handicapped child must have knowledge of early childhood development, skill in teaching normal as well as handicapped children, and a profound interest in learning from children. Emphasizing the need for more knowledge, Sidney P. Marland stated:

Among all the things educators admit to understanding only slightly is the process of learning itself. In this decade we are groping, with powerful allies from the field of child development, to learn more about learning . . . Inquiries into the way children learn have led to the following: . . . investigations into ways of stimulating the learning processes of the emotionally disturbed child, the child with cerebral dysfunction or brain damage, the under-achiever with a good mind not yet in motion. *Much more needs to be learned about how atypical children can be helped to learn*[8] (italics added).

The teacher of the multiply handicapped child must combine knowledge of the effects of handicapping conditions on child development with the ability to observe and record activity and behavior. A great deal has been written about the effects of motor sensory deficits, brain damage, the behavior of the emotionally disturbed child, and the learning process of the mentally retarded child, but this whole field is still in its infancy. At schools, hospitals, and clinics research on various handicapping conditions is being conducted by professional teams that include medical, psychological, and teaching personnel.

The teacher of these children should read widely in the field of special education and should have some knowledge of medical terms so that she can communicate with other professional person-

[8]Sidney P. Marland, Jr., "Ferment in the Schools," *Children* 12 (March-April 1965):66.

nel who are interested in her special work. She also needs this knowledge to deepen her understanding of the origins of various kinds of behavior, and to supplement her own observations, thus gaining a total picture of the functioning of multiply handicapped children.

The emphasis here is on the special role of the teacher, not only in the classroom situation but in the professional teamwork process of understanding how the atypical child learns. Her observations and recordings of the child's behavior and learning patterns are an invaluable mine of information. In some areas she also acts as a member of a diagnostic team. For example, children with physical defects may appear to be mentally retarded. It is often only after a period of time in a classroom that a diagnosis can be made.

There are certain attitudes that a teacher must avoid. Pity and solicitude are harmful to a child's developing self-concept. Janet Pomeroy explains, "Many handicapped persons have stated that of all the attitudes expressed toward them pity is the most despised. It involves devaluation even though the person expressing it may actually want to help . . . Solicitude is also a very common reaction, which is said, in many instances, to represent a strong effort to deny an unconscious rejection. The solicitude of parents and members of a family, or of anyone working with the physically handicapped can be a detriment to their total development. "[9]

A handicapped child reacts to pity and solicitude either by withdrawing into himself or by just giving up the struggle for independence. The child needs support, warmth, interest, concern, appreciation of his achievements, and respect for his personality. Feeling for the child must be combined with knowledge of the child.

According to Paul Lemkau: "The quality of sympathy and compassion is needed no less now than it was in the past. But there is new information to deal with, and there are new concepts to be applied in thinking about the effect of handicaps. Attitudes of sympathy need to be supplemented with interpretations from the scientific field that may make our compassion more effective in helping

[9]Pomeroy, *Recreation*, p. 15.

the handicapped person to achieve a more complete range of experience."[10]

There are a number of ways in which a teacher can give a child support. Nonverbal communication is important. The way in which a teacher takes a child by the hand when she walks with him from the bus to the classroom often sets the tone for the day. To gain a child's attention, a gentle touch on the shoulder while calling his name will often communicate warmth and interest.

Unacceptable behavior should not be rewarded with a great deal of attention. A child should quietly but firmly be removed from a group when he is indulging in a tantrum. But expression of frustration should be investigated so that the teacher can help a child overcome his frustration or learn to cope with his problems. These multiply handicapped children have many frustrations; they need help to understand what they can do and what is impossible for them. Also, the child should learn what is expected from him and what he can expect from his teacher. The teacher should be consistent in rewarding efforts and achievements, enabling the child to understand the teacher's behavior.

A teacher should not permit herself to become emotionally involved with the children. At all times she must strive to maintain her role as a teacher. When the multiply handicapped child enters an educational program he is still dependent on his mother and other adults. This dependence may last to some degree for the rest of his life.

But the entire educational program is geared to helping the child achieve his full stature. When he first comes into the school he will transfer some of his emotional dependence to his teacher. To some extent he will be physically dependent on her while he is learning motor skills and the activities of daily living. As the teacher helps him with some of his physical needs, the child learns that there is another adult outside his family on whom he can rely. This may help the teacher win his trust and confidence. In some areas the teacher serves as a mother; at the same time she still must maintain her role as a teacher.

The teacher should help the child achieve emotional as well as physical independence. She must, therefore, be sensitive and

[10]Lemkau, "Influence of Handicapping Conditions," p. 43.

knowledgeable enough to know how, and when to give the child any help he needs. With physical maturation and independence, the normal child moves away from emotional dependence, out of the family and toward the world. But *the multiply handicapped child must achieve emotional independence and maturity while he is still physically dependent on his mother and other adults.*

Teacher and Parent

Although a teacher does not function as a parent and the parent does not become a teacher, still each has a somewhat dual role. In her classroom the teacher must provide the warmth and concern that are ordinarily associated with a mother's role. But the special education teacher of young multiply handicapped children does not merely teach academic skills. She helps the child experience life—helps him to grow, helps to motivate him to explore his environment—and part of the effort to accomplish these goals is the creation of a warm, accepting environment where the child feels free to explore and interested enough to explore.

A teacher may pick up a child and take him over to a window to look out at a snow storm. She teaches the children how to take off their coats and how to put on their hats. These are skills that a child usually learns from his mother.

The responsibility of the special education teacher does not end with the child. She also helps to guide the parent. She shares her expertise by meeting with the parent and explaining what she is doing at school. Thus, at home each new step in growth is reinforced and becomes a part of the child. This relates not to the actual teaching of skills. That is, if a child is learning to take off his cap and put it in a cubicle, the teacher informs the parent and asks only that the child be expected to take off his cap and hang it up at home.

When a child does not become overly stimulated when his parents visit the classroom, they should be invited to visit and observe again. If this is not possible because of the child's poor reaction, the teacher should meet with the parents to explain her methods and goals as well as the child's progress.

Although parent-teacher contacts and conferences are necessary in all phases of education, there is a special need for them when working with the multiply handicapped child. There is the danger that a teacher may become a surrogate mother or father. This confusion of roles does not help the child, the parent, or the teacher. By maintaining close contact with the parent, the teacher keeps her own role in clear focus and makes a more effective contribution to the child's growth. Parent and teacher can learn from each other. Together they can work out a consistent approach to the child.

The Teacher and the Team

As has been mentioned, the young multiply handicapped child is usually serviced by more professionals than just his classroom teacher. If he is learning to walk with braces, he is seen by a physical therapist. If he needs help with speech, he is seen by a speech therapist. The teacher is concerned not with one particular area of disability, but with the child's total functioning. For that reason it is important that the specialists relate to the teacher. Whatever skills are being developed in individual therapy must be discussed with the teacher so that she can incorporate them into her own work with the child. For example, if the physical therapist is teaching a child to hop on crutches, the teacher must be informed, so that when the child goes to the toilet he is permitted to hop with his crutches.

Or perhaps a child is being seen by a psychologist, who rewards acceptable behavior with pretzels and ginger ale. In order to guarantee carry-over the teacher should be informed, and when the child finishes a puzzle he might be rewarded with ginger ale and pretzels.

Similarly, the teacher should relate the child's classroom functioning to the other specialists. Whenever possible, consultants should work in the classroom. The speech therapist can help develop a language environment there, in addition to working with children on an individual basis. A psychologist who is helping to train teachers in behavior modification techniques surely needs to work in the classroom.

Summary

The basic classroom staff is composed of the teacher, her assistant, and an aide. These three implement the program. The teacher trains her assistants to work with the children.

The role of the special education teacher is many faceted. In addition to structuring a program that meets the individual needs of the multiply handicapped child, the teacher must also relate to and integrate the other specialists working with the child. And finally, she needs to work with parents in such a way that parent and teacher mutually support each other in their work with the child.

Chapter **4**

THE PROGRAM

The following program is a compilation of techniques used with multiply handicapped children in two different schools. In one (a residential school) the primary handicap was blindness and the secondary handicap was cerebral palsy. In the other (a day school) the primary handicap was mental retardation and the secondary handicap was emotional disturbance. In both settings, the children had many additional handicaps. For example, in the school for blind children a nine-year-old blind girl had cerebral palsy, a hearing loss, retarded speech, petit mal seizures, and an I.Q. of 53. Her primary handicap was diagnosed as blindness only so that she could be placed in a school for the blind. Were there a school available for children with cerebral palsy that would take a blind child, her primary handicap might be classified as cerebral palsy. Often the diagnosis of a primary handicap may depend on the type of facility that is available. In this case, the basic diagnosis should have been "multiple handicaps."

The following curriculum grew out of work with children with multiple problems. It is hoped that teachers will find some areas of this program useful for children with various disabilities.

Ages and Grouping

The ages of multiply handicapped children in an early childhood program may range from four to nine. The chronological age often has little relationship to the maturation age. Multiply handicapped children have an erratic development; they function on different levels of motor, language, and emotional and intellectual development. Their wide range of development calls for many adaptations to meet individual needs as well as the over-all needs of a group. Some of the nine-year-old children will be too mature for some phases of this program, whereas many four-year-olds will not be ready for a number of the activities. The teacher adapts activities to meet the children's mental and physical needs, as well as their level of social maturity.

The optimum number of children in a group varies with the kind of activity. For activities held outdoors or on trips away from school, the ideal child-adult ratio is one-to-one in order to guarantee the children's safety and sense of security. For trips one can make use of parents or volunteers. A singing group can contain up to ten children with a teacher and aide. For classroom work a teacher works best with approximately four children in a group and a maximum of eight children in her class. Some examples of grouping are described below:

The Home Group

The children should be assigned to a home group after a period of observation by the team. The assignment should be based on the over-all functioning of the child and the functioning level of the children in his peer group. A child's competence in the general areas of self-care, communication, gross and fine motor coordination, socialization, and perceptual skills should be carefully observed and assessed before assignment to a home group.

The child's home room or group is where he comes in the morning and leaves from in the afternoon. He also eats and rests there. Most of his time is spent with this group, but he may go to other groups for special needs. Sometimes the breakdown into activity groups takes place in his home room, although in some schools it is possible to form special activity groups from several home classes.

Activity Grouping

The home group is the stable base, but there should be regrouping for special activities. Special needs may include motor exercises, music, dancing, and optometric exercises. For work with materials the children should be grouped according to their needs by their home room teacher. Work with materials may include preacademic materials, arts and crafts materials, or seat work for eye-hand coordination. Children should be moved along according to their own level of development, not according to the group's progress. Therefore, the teacher should work with the children at their table; she rarely should stand in front of the room. The emphasis should be on highly individualized teaching. Each child should have an individualized program—a "prescription for education" written by the team, carried out by the teacher and consultants, and then evaluated by the team.

Grouping Children with Behavior Problems

Unless a child has severe emotional problems and is so aggressive that he is a danger to himself and others, generally he can be contained within his functional peer group. Not all children with emotional problems should be placed in a so-called emotionally disturbed group. Such a child needs contact with better adjusted children. Where this mixed grouping has been tried, with the disturbed child receiving special attention within the group, he has often made contact with the other children after a period of time.

Physical Development

Most multiply handicapped children have retarded motor development. They crawl, stand, and walk later than other children. Many of them are quite awkward in their movements. They have not learned how to use their bodies, and they may have little understanding of themselves as physical beings. They need help in learning to walk, run, hop, skip, jump, or generally to move through space and to explore the environment.

Some period during each day should be devoted to physical exercise. Children should learn how to roll on a mat. Perhaps at first a child may need help from a teacher who can gently propel him so that he rolls over, until he learns to roll by himself. Jumping, rolling, hopping—all the large motor movements are what a child should learn.

The classroom should have a climbing apparatus, a barrel, and a small slide. A special room for a gym is most desirable. In outdoor playgrounds the children should be encouraged to go on swings, climb jungle gyms, walk on logs, and go up and down the slides.

Through this emphasis on motor development, the children learn not only how to use their bodies for particular activities, but also how to move through space. The child who is learning to walk with crutches, or wearing braces, or using a wheel chair should also participate in the indoor and outdoor physical activities. Although the motor development always will be limited by the physical handicap, walking outdoors on crutches or maneuvering a wheel chair gives a child independence in moving through space.

In a school for multiply handicapped children one may assume that a number of children need physical therapy. This is a particular need of the young child with cerebral palsy. However, it is difficult to take a child out of his group for individual physical therapy. And a school is hardly an ideal clinical setting. There are a number of ways in which this therapy can be handled. The two proposals below are based on experience in programs for the multiply handicapped:

1. A physical therapist serves as a consultant. She visits the school once a week and trains the teacher in a simple range of motion exercises—heel cord stretching, walking in parallel bars, etc. She checks the child's skills, observes the teacher, and suggests new exercises. If a child is being seen in an out-patient clinic, the school therapist checks with the physical therapist to make sure the school is following the same routine.

2. There is a physical therapist on the staff who takes full responsibility for the therapy. She does the individual therapy, checks with the clinics, etc.

Whether one uses one method or the other depends on the needs of the children and the school's total curriculum. But even when there is a large number of children in need of physical therapy, rather than take them out of their group it may be possible to arrange for the parents to take their children to a clinic after school hours.

In other situations it may be necessary for the school to have all the therapies available in the school facility. In any case, whatever the child learns in the physical therapy setting, whether in the school or the clinic, the teacher must be informed. It is her responsibility to incorporate the therapy "lessons" into the general curriculum. When a child makes use of his lessons in daily life, he recognizes the meaning of what he has learned.

For example, if a child is being taught reciprocal motion by a therapist, it will have much greater meaning for him if his class teacher helps him to crawl over to a ball or a brightly colored doll. Similarly, a child will be more highly motivated to walk with crutches if he uses them to go to the bathroom instead of having to be pushed in a wheelchair. And children who are learning to walk up and down stairs can practice right in their classroom as part of a game or during the free play period.

In order to function as part of a team, the teacher must be kept informed of all developments so that she can reinforce in her program all the child's new experiences.

Moving Through Space

The normal, young child, as he creeps and crawls and stumbles about his house, is experimenting with space. For example, he may crawl over to a table, feel one of the legs, and then carefully pull himself up. Once he is erect and can look over the top of the table, a beatific grin will spread all over his face. Or he may toddle over to a rocker, steady it with one hand, climb into it, and then rock back and forth—lord of all he surveys. In both cases the child changed his body position, learned something of the properties of objects, and found that he could manage his environment and enlarge his own "space."

These are the experiences to which one must expose the multiply handicapped child. For motivation this child needs support, opportunity, and guidance.

In her classroom the teacher can construct a simple maze which facilitates the above experiences. The child can be motivated to go through the maze by having the teacher go through with him, by watching the other children go through, and by a reward at the end of the maze.

The maze is an obstacle course which might include automobile tires, rails, inclines, platforms, and diagrams on the floor for positioning and color discrimination. For example, a maze routine might include: walking on a rail, stepping into and out of a box, crawling under a table, crawling through a barrel, and punching a ball suspended from the ceiling. The reward at the end might be either applause, a candy, or a hug.

Variations in a maze are endless. It can be simplified or made more complex as the children master its parts.

There are many learning experiences inherent in the maze. The child learns about objects in space and about his body and body movements in space. He learns that he can crawl under and over some objects, and through others. With his own body he learns about the properties of these objects. He also learns that there is a relationship between his body movements and the objects. For instance, if he places one foot in front of the other in a certain manner, he can maintain his balance on a board. He also learns that there is a progression from one activity to another—that after walking on a board he comes to, say, a box—and that each object calls for a change in his body activity. He learns to change his body motion to achieve a result. For example, if he bends down, he can fit under a table.

A child also learns to wait his turn and to watch his classmates go through the maze. Finally, he learns that there is a beginning and an end to an activity.

Music and Physical Growth

Music should not be relegated simply to music periods. It should be used as a tool of growth in all areas—to motivate children to walk, run, climb stairs, skip, march, throw, catch, and jump. During the exercise period the teacher might provide music for marching, for lifting legs high in the air, for jumping from one spot to another, for swaying from side to side, or for moving up and down. The teacher can use records, play simple melodies on the piano, or simply beat a drum.

Summary

Recognizing that multiply handicapped children are retarded in developing motor skills and spatial concepts, the teacher must build physical activities into her curriculum. She should incorporate exercise, physical therapy, maze activity, and rhythmic music into her daily schedule.

The multiply handicapped child should be consciously guided by adults through activities that are otherwise not accessible to him. As James L. Hymes remarks, "The activities that provide [the multiply handicapped child] with a normal degree of maturation for his age are those things which the normal child at his age has already acquired."[11]

Play

Play can be "just physical activity, an overflow of energy, of exuberance. . . . play experiences . . . belong among the natural playful uses which a child makes of his body."[12] Play is also the child's method of achieving some mastery of his environment. In play a child uses his whole body and exercises his muscles. He experiments with language as he chants, shouts, and sings. Through interaction with other children he learns something about himself and takes his first steps as a social being. In dramatic play he acts out his fears, anxieties, and observations. He reshapes and reconstructs his environment. Through play with their peers children begin to develop relationships beyond their families.

Multiply handicapped children need to play, but adults must provide support, participation, and structure for them. These children can not initiate play activities with others. They live within themselves. They play with their own bodies, or at most invent imaginary playmates. The teacher must motivate the children and adapt play activities to their needs.

[11] James L. Hymes, "Moving Toward Maturity," *Children* 7 (May-June 1960):111.
[12] *Ibid.*

Play as a Means of Learning about Space

The nonhandicapped child easily moves through space—he walks, hops, jumps, and runs. He learns to walk up and down steps. Normal "children enter this period [of early childhood] having recently made dramatic gains in posture, balance and locomotion. They are, as a result, deeply involved in extending this new-found mastery of their bodies and seemingly filled with almost boundless energy."[13]

Multiply handicapped children can never achieve such mastery, but they can move through space in their own fashion by increasing control of their bodies.

With some help they can use most of the standard, outdoor recreational equipment. For example, to help a child down a slide one adult can carry or guide him to the top, while another stands at the foot ready to catch him as he slides down.

Children who have multiple sensory deficits but no orthopedic handicaps can be taught to use various clues to help them climb a jungle gym. For example, a child with visual and hearing losses can climb with the teacher, as she shows the child where to put his hands for the next rung. When they get to the top the teacher helps him extend his arms up into the air, indicating that there are no more rungs to climb. Then they climb down side by side, the teacher helping the child use his feet to find the rungs below.

Play and Sensory Stimuli

Into each day's activities the teacher should incorporate sensory experiences so that the child will become aware of his environment. In planning her day, the teacher might ask herself, "How will this activity reach the children?"

Water play, for example, is effective for tactile stimulation. And it is the rare child who does not enjoy such play. A water table filled with water and toys will arouse a child's interest and curiosity. The teacher can put detergent into the water and provide dolls to wash. She can pour coloring agents into the water and have the children watch as the water changes color. All kinds of floating toys—boats, ducks—can be used that children can push in the water. The chil-

[13] *Ibid.*

dren, as well as the teacher, should wear large, waterproof aprons. Sand play is another activity that exercises the sense of touch. A sand table, equipped with pails, shovels, sifters, and other sand toys, should be provided in a room for young multiply handicapped children. Digging in the sand with hands or shovels is an important tactile experience.

Active Games

Many active games can be adapted for use by the multiply handicapped (see Appendix). Games requiring teams encourage cooperation as well as competition among the children. And, of course, these games have a physically therapeutic value. The skills the children acquire so painfully at physical therapy sessions are used joyously as they crawl, hop, or race on crutches to reach a goal. Children with poor vision use auditory clues to locate themselves and others in space and readily follow verbal directions during a game. And it is all done with joy and exuberance.

In the excitement of a competitive game the children call out to each other, chant, squeal, and burst into spontaneous laughter and shouts of triumph. They are also capable of trying to cheat, or of complaining, "It's not fair!" In their own fashion they experience all the rough-and-tumble of early childhood.

They also learn how to function in a group and how to give each other support and assistance. They take their first steps in social living and cooperation as they play together and compete against each other. They also learn how to take turns and how to "be a good sport" and accept defeat.

Games also help the children build realistic self-concepts and images of their playmates. A child learns that he can move relatively quickly on crutches as he observes another child crawling on all fours. When a blind child picks up the shout of a teammate and can then run toward him, he has learned to use his hearing to get about in space. Games are thus used to stimulate the children to use their senses and bodies to explore the environment.

Outdoor Play

School should be held outdoors. The whole world is the classroom for the multiply handicapped child. Children should go outdoors in all kinds of weather. Many children have been so isolated that they haven't walked in the rain or rolled in the snow. Children should experience the sun and the wind, the rain, and the snow. Collecting leaves, or scooping up snow and watching it melt are meaningful nature lessons.

The teacher can structure her schedule so that there is an outdoor period each day—sometimes for playground activity, at other times for nature lessons.

Singing Games

A number of years ago an exhibition of photographs, entitled "The Family of Man," portrayed children of many lands, different ages, different skin colors—all playing the same kinds of games. There were the children clasping hands, and going around in a circle—in Italy, China, the United States, Japan, the Soviet Union, and elsewhere.

Singing games are the universal and timeless legacy of children, including the multiply handicapped. These children may not be able to perform as well as the nonhandicapped, but they can adapt to singing games. Some of them can stand in a circle, and some can even walk around by holding on to their wheelchairs.

They all can play "Did You Ever See a Lassie?" The teacher helps a child with involved limbs go through the motions. She describes the motions to the child who cannot see. She stands with a physically handicapped child to give him support. The children are not concerned with their handicaps; they are so involved in the singing games that often they find their own solutions to physical limitations. Like all children, they love the singing, clapping, and chanting together. There is a kind of magic in the singing game. Adults are accepted in the game, but only as part of the background.

The list of singing games which can be adapted for use by multiply handicapped children is long and varied (see Appendix). Often the children will introduce a new version of an old game, add their own jingle, or make up their own nonsense rhymes. Singing games give the children release from their strictured physical world. They can experiment with sounds and words, and break out of the bounds of formal language to experience the joy of creating.

Block Play

Block building, which is an important experience for normal children, may have limited meaning for some multiply handicapped children. A teacher must be careful that she does not routinely introduce block building simply because it is part of the early childhood program. Multiply handicapped children when first exposed to a rich, stimulating environment, are so involved in exploring their terrain that they are not interested in materials which do not say anything to them about their surroundings. Most of these multiply handicapped young children are first attracted to objects that either make sounds, have bright colors, or have some intriguing tactile covering. The teacher must therefore evaluate whether a child needs block building to further his progress. Has he arrived at the stage where he can profit from block building? Is placing one block on top of another going to help in achieving coordination? Will the child be interested in building a house and perhaps placing dolls in the house to reproduce a family living situation?

When a child is ready for blocks, the teacher must at first take an active part in the building and be sure that the experience does not frustrate the child. He may destroy a tower with one uncoordinated move of his hands. When a child does become involved in working with blocks, the benefits he derives are meaningful and varied. He becomes thoroughly absorbed. His attention span is increased and his ability to concentrate is strengthened. The child with involved hands exerts tremendous self-discipline to keep his hands steady.

Block building is also an important social experience for multiply handicapped children. Two children with different handicaps may build together and they learn how to cooperate to achieve a common end. A child with good hands might pile the blocks on top of each other, while another child might go to the shelves and bring the supplies. While working they might discuss their building concepts and impressions.

In manipulating blocks the children are placing objects in space. They learn that a smaller block can fit on a larger one and that the reverse will not work. This is an important learning experience. Many of the children try to manipulate their environment with tears and tantrums. But by building with blocks they will learn that there are natural laws which cannot be manipulated.

Dramatic Play

The normal child gives vent to his fears, angers, and frustrations in dramatic play. He reconstructs his world by taking on the role of the powerful adult or by playing the part of the small and helpless child in need of protection. He acts out situations which have bewildered and hurt him.

By acting out different roles the child learns to cope with a frightening reality. He puts the experience in terms that are understandable to him. A child's meaning is often different from an adult's meaning. What a child cannot verbalize he may be able to act out.

Alert teachers can often find out more about a child's feelings by watching his "play" than by any other means.

Young multiply handicapped children develop their own ways of acting out their fears and restructuring their environment: they fantasize; they withdraw from threatening experiences; they perseverate; they balk at any change.

The teacher looks for better ways for them to act out their fears or desires. Knowing something of a child's experiences, she can set the stage to guide him toward acting out his own particular life experiences. She provides an environment that the child can control, and she helps him to understand this environment.

Playing House

A doll corner is standard nursery school equipment; it is equally necessary in the program for multiply handicapped children, although it is used differently.

The doll corner should include dolls that speak and walk, and a baby doll that can take a bottle. The doll corner also should be equipped with a shelf of toys that make sounds—jewelry boxes that play music when they are opened, a clock with a musical chime, etc. To play house they need toys to motivate them and an adult to participate and take on roles herself. The teacher usually initiates the play by taking the girls over to the doll corner. She gives them the dolls to hold, shows them how to give a baby a bottle, pulls the cord that makes one of the dolls talk. She gives the children the various toys that make sounds, and helps them investigate all the furniture and equipment in the housekeeping corner.

Only after a time will the children take over the actual acting out of home situations. There are probably a number of reasons for this. The children are so isolated from the life of their families that they really don't know what roles the mother and father have in the house. Or it may be that they are aware that they cannot fulfill the role of a mother in caring for a child, so they are fearful of trying. Then too, at first they don't know how to play together in an unstructured situation; they can't put the pieces together. But in time they develop their own play patterns, and the dramatic play is then most revealing of their feelings and concepts.

Dramatic Play

A teacher can make use of dramatic play to deepen a child's awareness of his environment. For example, in the school for blind children one of the main forms of dramatic play for many of the multiply handicapped children was "going to the clinic." In their play the children would pretend to get on a bus or into a car with their parents. Then they would get off the bus at a special entrance to a hospital, pretend to go through a lobby of the hospital, and ride up in the elevator until they arrived at the floor of the doctor's office. Then would come the acting out of the visit. After the doctor's visit, the children would go to the therapist for exercises. Another version of "going to the clinic" might be a visit to the speech and hearing clinic for testing. Whatever version the children played involved a trip in some vehicle.

From such play it is possible to develop a unit on transportation. In listening to the children it becomes apparent that they take modes of transportation for granted. Wherever they go they have to use some means of transportation, and from their earliest days they have been accustomed to being taken from one place to another. Yet they have little curiosity about the various modes of travel. Since many agencies pay for their transportation, often they are not aware that it costs money to travel by bus or by plane. To help them become more aware of various means of transportation and more observant on their trips, the game "Going on a Trip" can be used.

The game starts with a child choosing the kind of trip he wants to make—a visit to grandparents, a trip to see a brother in basic training, a trip for a vacation, and so on. He decides where he wants to go and how to get there. Other children are encouraged to suggest alternative ways of getting to the destination. This easily can lead to a general discussion on various modes of travel.

Once this topic has been thoroughly exhausted, the game progresses to the preparation for a trip. This discussion includes such items as who buys the tickets and how much is paid for different trips. This is stated not in terms of dollars and cents, but rather in terms of relative costs of, say, a bus trip as compared to a trip by plane.

The final part of the game is a discussion of baggage. Each child adds an item to a list of things to take on a trip. The number of things to take along is determined by the kind of trip being discussed and all items must be things which are of actual use on such a trip.

From these games the children learn that one pays for transportation and that they receive financial support from agencies. They discuss the different sounds made by motors, or the way they feel when a plane ascends. They learn the titles of the people who drive the different vehicles—the bus driver, the train engineer, the airplane pilot. They learn which is the fastest mode of travel and discuss their preferences in transportation.

The game "Going on a Trip" should be used as a starting point for discussion. The teacher guides the game by listening to the children's ideas on travel and by asking questions to help them clarify and understand their experiences. As a result of these discussions, the children will be much more aware and observant on their next trip.

Through structured play activities the children learn to locate themselves and others in space, and to appreciate some of the properties of space. They also develop their motor skills, and learn to use their bodies. Through games which stress visual, auditory, and tactual clues they begin to make better use of their unimpaired senses. They build self-concepts based on their sense of achievement and understanding of their capacities.

Although they remain dependent on adults for some forms of emotional support and physical help, they learn to rely on themselves and their peers to a greater degree for play enjoyment. Through play they become part of a community of children. No longer is the family the sole center of their universe. Like normal children, they begin to turn outward for some of their gratification. Complete dependence on the mother is finally broken.

Play has special significance in the learning and growth of the multiply handicapped child. Much of his life is necessarily built on discipline and control. He must learn, often painfully, how to control his body and make use of his unimpaired senses. Play is the area where he learns freely and joyously. Planned play in school should not be confined to the early years of childhood. These children develop on several levels at extremely different growth rates. Their need for play must, therefore, be interpreted in the light of their specific, unique, total development. However, it is in early childhood that the basis should be laid for later riches and happiness.

Free Play

Multiply handicapped children, for the most part, can tolerate only brief periods of free play. In the morning, before the day's routine begins, and possibly after nap time there can be brief periods when the children may explore the room or perhaps have access to toys. They should be given these opportunities under supervision, since most of them do not know what to do when left to themselves. The teacher introduces them to free play by giving them familiar toys. Simply to set these children loose during free play is often a disservice since they become bewildered. With help they learn how to use the time. This process contributes to their development, because ultimately they appreciate the value of skills acquired in structured situations. When they have learned to ride a tricycle, to push and pull toys, or to play with cars, they can use free time more effectively and independently.

Creative Activities

"That creative activities serve as a means for emotional release and adjustment, that they promote the independence and flexibility of thinking, that they can be used for group dynamics and social interaction, has not yet penetrated the thick walls of most of our institutions. Happiness apparently is still a luxury which handicapped people cannot afford in a materialistic time, in which the education of the handicapped is almost exclusively geared toward preparation for making a living."[14] Viktor Lowenfeld thus expressed concern for the narrow view held by some schools for creative activities.

Teachers of handicapped children are using the creative arts in their work, but this effort is usually regarded as a frill by the administration. There is little understanding of the role of creative experiences in the education of multiply handicapped children. Schools for these children have traditionally been preoccupied with the management of the children in school, and the aim has been to equip the children with vocational skills, rather than to accommodate their basic needs. Too little attention has been paid to the total development of the child into a well-rounded individual with resources for living a full life. In too many areas the emphasis has been on training, not on education.

"With the blind child, as well as with the seeing, creative aesthetic expression is the most important phase of human existence, as well as the phase most neglected."[15] This sentence, quoted from Thomas Cutsforth's book on the blind, was written in 1932. Fifteen years later, Viktor Lowenfeld pointed out that the handicapped child was still being denied the experience of creative living. The emphasis today is still on rehabilitation and on helping the child to become merely a self-supporting, well-mannered member of society.

This lack of understanding of the role of creative arts in the development of young multiply handicapped children only reflects society's attitudes toward education of handicapped children. Art

[14]Viktor Lowenfeld, *Creative and Mental Growth* (New York: Macmillan Co., 1957), p. 431.
[15]Thomas D. Cutsforth, *The Blind in School and Society* (New York: American Foundation for the Blind, 1951), p. 193.

is not practical, it is said. How can music, art, literature, poetry, dance, and dramatics help the handicapped person make a living? The answer is that the creative arts are designed not to give one a vocational skill, but to enrich the lives of all human beings. To deny these experiences to the multiply handicapped child is to stunt his growth and to deprive him of one of the most powerful forces we have for molding personality.

Music

We start with music because it is the universal language of humanity. Just try to imagine a world without music. It is inconceivable. Music is all around us. We even speak with music, in our use of inflection, tone, and accent to give life to our way of speaking. Music has many meanings: a shared musical experience creates bonds between people; for some it provides an escape into another world. Music also awakens the senses to new experiences, extends the horizons of living, adds depth and meaning to experience. Music itself is an experience in living.

In the curriculum music includes songs and rhythms—listening to the classics, learning to play rhythm instruments, singing, and dancing. For some of the children it also may mean learning to play the piano. Music permeates the day.

Songs

In singing together children share a delightful and joyous learning experience. There are songs for opening the day, for different seasons of the year, and for welcoming new children and guests. Folk songs are particularly appealing to children; a repertoire of folk songs creates a bond between handicapped and nonhandicapped children. Negro spirituals, sea chanteys, and folk songs of other lands add depth and emotion to the children's lives. Songs express every emotion, and are a form of release for children. To help them discover humor there is nothing quite like nonsense songs. Children with speech defects can learn to sing. Those who stutter may be able to sing sweetly without error.

Once handicapped children have learned to sing, they begin to make up their own words to melody, just as other children do. And what a delight it is for a child to hear a song made up about him. To help a child develop a positive feeling about himself there is little that is quite as effective as describing him in song. Even disturbed, withdrawn children can be brought into the magic circle of singing children, because music is a humanizing experience. As they sing they shed many of their inhibitions, and carry the music with them as they go through the day.

Once these children have learned to sing together and have built a repertoire of songs, they have a new form of group communion. They can now initiate an activity by themselves without the intervention of an adult. Instead of always waiting for an adult to bring them together, they can and do use singing during their free time. They now have a new form of group play and communication.

"It is wrong to assume that a child can be taught music before he has experienced it."[16] After the children have had their own experiences in making music, the teacher can introduce records of great singing voices. There are no limits to how far a child's love of music can be developed, but all learning begins with the child's own experiences. For example, one teacher of mentally retarded children with other handicaps used music as the basis for her whole morning's activities. The six children in her group were four and one-half to six years of age. In addition to severe retardation, some of the other disabilities included cerebral palsy, epilepsy, and autism. None of these children had oral language ability.

The day's schedule began with a good morning song, sung to each child by the teacher and her assistant. The children were seated in a circle. One of the children was taken by the hand and walked around the circle. As each child's name was mentioned in the song the child who was walking around the circle would stop and shake hands. Or instead, as each child's name was mentioned in the song a mirror would be placed in front of him.

On some occasions the morning singing circle might be followed by taking the children over to the standing table, and having them stand in their slots. The teacher would go to each with a box of rhythm instruments, from which the child would choose one—a

[16]Eleanor W. Thayer, "Music, Kindergarten Through the Elementary Grades," *American Association of Instructors for the Blind* (June 1950), pp. 172-175.

bell or a tambourine. Then with background music playing on the phonograph, the teacher would go from child to child and show him how to use his instrument. Sometimes she would attract a child's vision by shaking a tambourine above his head, and then moving the tambourine in an arc. The child would follow the sound with his eyes and move his head to watch the movements of the tambourine.

These were some of the ways in which music was used to help children come out of themselves and focus on their surroundings. These were techniques used with sound and music to stimulate awareness of the environment.

Singing Through the Day

Morning songs can be used to begin each day. They can be about the season of the year or the morning. Such songs are found in any good song book. A great favorite is "Oh, What a Beautiful Morning." Often a teacher may introduce a new song and teach it during the morning circle, rather than during the regular singing period. This informal approach to teaching songs helps to make singing a natural part of the children's lives.

While outdoors, musical activities are often appropriate. It is delightful to take a harmonica outdoors, or to sing in a group when some of the children are tired of playing. The teacher may start to sing while a group is going for a walk; the children will join in easily and naturally.

Singing periods are, nevertheless, important. The children learn through rote memorization and spontaneous imitation. The teacher introduces a song by playing it on the piano and singing it for the children. Then she goes over each phrase repeatedly with them until they all know the words. Then each child gets a chance to sing a solo. It is during these periods that the teacher introduces the children to a wide repertoire of songs. Some periods can then be completely devoted to "choosing time"—each child picks a favorite song for the group to sing.

Trips away from school provide good singing opportunities. When leaving on a trip the teacher starts by singing good-bye to the school. That is generally all she needs to do. The children will sing the rest of the way. If they have a large repertoire of songs, one child after another will suggest a new song. They will sing the songs they learned at school, and those they have heard on the radio or on records. They are free to choose what they desire.

Improvising Words to Songs

The teacher takes a familiar folk song and improvises words which describe the children in an amusing light. For example, she may sing:

"Last night I had the strangest dream
I'd ever dreamed before.
I dreamed that all the children here
Were sleeping on the floor."

Children will think of numerous situations and improvise rhymes about themselves, the teacher, their families, and their classmates.

Another method for helping the children to rhyme is to say a few words about a child, describing his appearance, and then to ask the children to guess who it is. The children can then go on to make up their own rhyming puzzles to music.

Rhythm and Movement

Multiply handicapped children can be taught to move their bodies to music. At first an adult will have to take them physically through the motions of swaying or bending to music. Children with poor posture and sitting balance are motivated by the music to sit up straight and to keep their heads still. Many multiply handicapped children have habits of rocking from side to side, keeping their heads down, or biting their wrists. Through learning to move to music, they are helped to overcome some of these habits.

The teacher plays an ascending and descending scale to illustrate the ordered progressions of tones and the difference between high notes and low notes. The children raise and lower their arms as the music goes up and down the scale.

Music is played for running, skipping, hopping, and walking

slowly or quickly. In this way the children begin to respond to music. Those who can crawl may get down on the floor and move in time to the music. Those who cannot crawl clap in time to the rhythm. They may become galloping horses by clapping on their thighs, birds by moving their arms, or elephants by raising and lowering their legs slowly and heavily to the rhythm of the music. Children who can stand with support hold on to the back of a chair, raising and lowering their legs in time to the music. Children who cannot stand go through the same motions while seated.

Severely handicapped children cannot improvise motions to music as normal children can, because their rhythmic experiences need a great deal of guidance and physical assistance. But those children who have an innate sense of rhythm can learn to move to music. The tempo of a march tells them how to march on crutches to the beat. Children in wheel chairs can learn to turn the wheels of their chairs and "dance" in their wheel chairs in perfect time to the music. Children with mild physical handicaps can be paired with adults, and learn some of the simple figures of the square dance. While some children square dance, others may clap in unison to the rhythm of the music. For children with a pitching gait it is possible to improvise dances that are built on their particular mode of locomotion; the possible adaptations are endless.

Through moving to music these children learn to make better use of their bodies. The handicaps do not impose such severe restrictions that the children cannot learn to enjoy their bodies, but they need the help and guidance of adults. Instead of focusing on what they can't do physically, the children concentrate on what they can do and enjoy themselves in the process.

Rhythm Instruments

Playing rhythm instruments provides many kinds of learning experiences. When a child acts on an instrument he gets a sound response. The different sounds usher in a whole new world of auditory experience. These sounds can be either noise or music, depending on the control of the instrument. The motivation to learn this control is fired by playing the instruments, listening to melodies played on the piano, and hearing how the rhythm instrument accents the melodies. Playing rhythm instruments together to make music is a joyous group experience.

The teacher illustrates the difference between noise and music by first striking the piano keys arbitrarily with both hands, and then by playing the notes of a simple melody. She asks the children to listen for the loud notes and to clap each time they hear them. When she is sure that the children have grasped the beat and are keeping time to the music, she gives them their first rhythm instrument—the sticks. She explains that these sticks are like their hands and can be brought together in the same way.

The children are introduced to different rhythms by listening to marches, waltzes, polkas, mazurkas, etc. They may be introduced to the different rhythm of an Indian war dance, or the simple, powerful rhythm of the rhumba. Each time a child is given an instrument, the teacher first plays a melody on the piano and then uses the instrument to illustrate the tempo. A child with poor breath control gets a bird whistle. One with poor hand coordination gets a triangle, and one who may use his hands to tear buttons off his clothes gets the castanets. In each case the child gets the instrument which forces him to exert the greatest discipline.

Rhythm instruments produce an infinite variety of sounds. Music is the organization of sounds in patterns of pitch and rhythm. This is the structure children discover for themselves as they strike their instruments slowly or quickly. They produce loud and soft notes. The sound of the sand block is vastly different from that of the triangle. By experimenting with the instruments the children learn that the sand blocks, triangles, drums, bells, etc., can produce sounds of great variety and richness.

Experimentation with sound is only the beginning of this musical experience. In order to produce music it is imperative to pay attention—to hold oneself in readiness to strike a note when the music calls for it. Severely involved children can learn to hold and strike the instrument exactly on cue. They exert self-discipline in order to participate in the making of music; they can become so wholly absorbed in this creative experience that they control their muscles. For children who have a very short attention span this concentration on music can be carried over into other learning situations.

Making music together is a communal experience of tremendous emotional satisfaction. Children learn that through music they can express their own emotions. Making music also teaches mastery of the environment. The children control the instruments. It is because of their actions on an object that beautiful sounds are produced; without them the instruments are silent.

Special Musical Aptitudes

Even among multiply handicapped children, one may find some individuals who have special aptitudes. As a result of her music program, the teacher may find that one or two children have excellent abilities to distinguish one note from another. During the music period she should use the names of the notes in the scale, and then ask the children to name the notes as she plays them. One or two children in the group may be able to learn to name each note just by hearing it. The next step with these children would be to ask them to name the notes in the melodies they know. The teacher would play them as they say the names of the notes. These children even might be able to progress to the point where they can name notes on which to build new melodies.

This lesson would not be part of a regular music period for the group as a whole, but the teacher always should be aware that even in a multiply handicapped group there may be a child with some special ability to be developed.

Listening to Music

A musical education for these deprived children should include special time for "going to a concert" in the classroom—that is, listening to the music of great composers. There are wonderful children's records that include an introduction to the instruments of the orchestra. With their own knowledge of the different rhythm instruments, the children can more readily understand the instruments of the orchestra.

By listening to the music of the great composers and learning about their lives, they associate the music with the person. Music deepens their perception and their feelings about the environment.

They hear the roll of thunder, the fall of raindrops, the sounds of the countryside, and the noises of the city. But in music they hear their own emotions expressed, and so they move out of themselves, away from their solitary existences, to make common bonds with humanity.

Often even a withdrawn, hostile child can be intrigued and brought out of himself through the magic of musical experiences. Once he enters this realm his capacity for growth—for developing his own inner resources, for making contact with other children and with his environment—is immeasurably enhanced.

Children with brain damage often cannot tune out irrelevant stimuli. Their sense of hearing picks up all the auditory stimuli in the environment. They have to learn to achieve the kind of integration of the environment which will make it possible for them to concentrate on what they need to hear. Here, too, learning about music and listening to it can be of inestimable value. The child concentrates on hearing the important sound of the moment, and learns to place other sounds in the background.

Handicapped children cannot be introduced to formal learning of the skills with the ordinary methods. Teachers have to use every possible resource to interest and motivate them. Music serves not only this purpose; it also is a basis for acquiring a positive attitude toward learning, improving coordination, and strengthening the receptivity of the senses and the ability to express reactions. The use of music incorporates the concepts of training and begins the education that prepares children for a later, more structured school environment where many more demands will be made of them.

Arts and Crafts

Normal children are busily engaged from early childhood in imitating and restructuring their environment. They also reduce the world to their size and refashion it in their own image. Every child, in recreating his environment, is a tiny creator of a universe. In the sandbox he makes pies, lays out paths and roads, builds houses, and fashions people and animals. He collects rocks and builds houses. In the nursery school and kindergarten programs, he delights in manipulating materials. He rolls and pats and squeezes clay. He experiments with making shapes. With paint, clay, and crayons he begins to represent his surroundings. Through his representations he gives indications about himself—how he sees himself and others. With his art the normal child brings order into his world; he clarifies his feelings and his concepts.

This direct creative experience is not possible for the multiply handicapped child. Creative art experiences come after a long period of exposure to work with structured materials. The art life of the multiply handicapped child begins with crafts. Because art is representation—a form of symbolization—it can be introduced only after a number of preliminary experiences with concrete materials.

The multiply handicapped child, confronted with new materials, which do not give him a clue as to their puspose, might be quite frightened. He has no background of experience to bring to these materials. He isn't yet interested in representing an environment which he is only beginning to explore. Therefore, his art experience should begin with concrete materials with evident purpose.

For example, endless stringing of beads for coordination development becomes much more interesting for the child if he knows the beads will become a necklace for his teacher to wear during the day. Children also delight in making gifts to take home. Even children with severely involved hands can paste by using the whole palm, and that is all it takes to make a jewelry box for mother or a tile ashtray for father. The field is very rich in materials which these children can use. (See Appendix for materials and suggested projects.)

Things they make can be very simple but should be related to some important event. They can make birthday cards, or Christmas gifts for their parents. It may be only a box covered with shells that they pasted on. The importance is the giving of the gift they made.

Crafts is not just a busy activity. It is through crafts that multiply handicapped children can learn to work with purpose, with an end product in view. They discover that hands are tools for making objects. Their positive feelings about themselves are heightened as they produce something which they have made and which can give loved ones pleasure. Often for the first time, they are contributing. They are no longer just receiving. This sense of achievement is a giant step toward some forms of independence.

Creative Art

The basic principle underlying all art work with multiply handicapped children is to give them some means whereby they can represent their environment. By recreating with materials any part of this world, children draw closer to the environment. They become more involved with reality. They must think about their experiences in order to recreate them. They have to put together a picture of what they know and in the process solve many problems of space and relationships.

The multiply handicapped child who is partially sighted presents a very special problem. He has vision but not enough to function as well as the sighted child. He lives in a kind of twilight zone between the sighted and the blind, not really at home in either environment. Art is of special meaning to such a child; it gives him a method for clarifying his hazy concepts.

"The partially blind individual has, by the process of drawing, clarified his vague impression of nature. Through creative expression he has brought environment close to himself, an act which contributes greatly to help him overcome the feeling of isolation imposed upon him by his impaired sight."[17]

Following is the story of a young, partially sighted, emotionally disturbed boy and his experience with art:

Bobby was completely independent physically, and had articulate speech. He was skilled in games and could play the piano by ear. Yet he could not sit still. He jerked his head from side to side, and constantly talked to himself without using words. He made all kinds of noises when he was alone and when he was in a group. These noises were not really meaningless. They were part of his own code for acting out many personal and social conflicts in ways which he thought were unintelligible to others. He couldn't bear to be with other children, but he was unable to be by himself. When he went to the bathroom he urinated all over the walls. He didn't respond to any part of the program.

From the beginning Bobby liked to draw with crayons. His drawings were very immature and he used essentially the same picture —a house, a couple of trees, and two or three people. The house

[17]Lowenfeld, p. 465.

was a two-dimensional box. The people were drawn without details of fingers on hands, eyebrows, or hair. After drawing many of these pictures he began to draw himself during several activities at school. As he participated more in the school activities, his pictures contained more detail and variety. However, most of his pictures had some element of hostility or aggression. He drew children with guns in their hands and riding on horses, or he depicted a child cutting down a tree in which birds were nesting.

After a period of time an easel was set up for him in a room where he worked all by himself without supervision. No demands were made, or any structures set up. When drawing with crayons, he was absorbed and quiet, and appeared completely relaxed. While painting, he made many noises and jumped about and called out to people not in the room. A teacher began to spend time with him. At first she had him continue to paint with little direction. Then she began to show him how to indicate perspective and how to use colors for certain effects.

Bobby and his teacher then began to use other materials to get certain effects. After he saw the results of following these directions, he become more and more eager to listen to suggestions and follow them. After several months of working with paints he learned to work quietly, completely intent on what he was doing. The jumping about and the noises ceased. He learned how to observe, how to copy, how to work with several media. He achieved a degree of skill that won the admiration of children and adults.

This boy was physically able to paint. His teacher was his guide, but he was able to implement his own ideas. In the beginning his drawings reflected his inner experiences. As he began to draw and paint life experiences he began to use his vision more effectively. He trained himself to observe since he wanted to be able to paint what he saw.

As he became more relaxed and more observant, he was able to come out of his isolation. He began to enjoy some experiences with other children. He then was able to respond to other parts of the program as well. Through painting he moved closer to his environment and closer to other children.

A partially sighted child can identify with such creative activity. He projects himself outward into the world which he then brings to life in his drawing and painting. Not only does he recreate his world, but he places himself within that world. All creative activity starts with the self: it is the individual who creates and his work reflects his experiences and his concepts of himself. Painting and drawing have meaning and value for the partially sighted child beyond that for the normal child. Through his paintings he begins to integrate the disparate elements of his visual world. He brings together his isolated, fragmentary pieces and unifies them into a whole. He depicts himself in relationship to the world around him, and expresses his feelings, his emotions, his concept of himself, and his relationships to others. The process of creation helps him to clarify his reality and begin to understand more of the meaning of his experiences.

There are many other lessons derived from this process. This is the beginning of representation—using figures to stand for people. Children "write" stories with pictures. This is the path by which many of them learn to write.

The multiply handicapped child who is cut off from his environment by motor and sensory losses needs a very concrete approach to art. The line between fantasy and reality is hazy for him. His art work, therefore, must be based on concrete experiences. And the materials which can best be used for the artistic creations of these children should be taken from the environment. He can understand these. They are still representative since the materials stand for other things: a twig can stand for a tree, or bits of a leaf for a whole leaf. Other materials can be more truly representative; hardened soap can represent a mound of snow, sawdust can represent grass, or a tiny figure supported by two bits of stick can represent a child on crutches. However, the event which is represented should be based on an actual occurrence in the life of the child.

Out in the Snow

Following is an example that may serve to illustrate the way in which the most severely handicapped children (there were six in this class) can participate in a creative activity.

For multiply handicapped children who have never experienced a snowfall, except by hearing about it or seeing it from a window, the first contact with snow is a tremendously exhilarating experience. There is no describing the enthusiasm, excitement, and wonder of that first snowfall.

When the teacher of this class first introduced the idea of creating pictures of being out in the snow, there was at first stunned silence. This lasted only a moment, and then began the questions: "How?" "Can I make myself on a sled?" "Can we make the snow coming down?"

The children were given a day to think over just what they wanted to show. Each child chose his own experience. The picture had to show what he or she had really done out in the snow.

The teacher showed them white cotton and hardened soap to let them choose the material they thought would best represent the snow. Some chose soap for the snow-covered ground, and cotton for the snowflakes falling from the sky, because they thought of snowflakes as soft, and snow on the ground as cold and hard. They chose their materials by sensation.

All the children included themselves in the scenes depicted. They made pictures of themselves on crutches, in wheelchairs, on sleds, or pushing another child in a wheelchair. For bare trees they used twigs, and for hedges pieces of leaves. They clothed their figures in material which resembled that of their own clothing!

After depicting the snow on the ground and the falling flakes, the children added their twigs, leaves, and finally their figures. This was their first attempt to place objects in space on a two-dimensional surface. They placed the figures on the ground in relationship to the trees and leaves, and to each other.

What did the children actually do in the process of creating this picture? They mixed detergent and water together, and then beat it with an eggbeater to make it fluffy. With big movements they spread the soap mixture over the heavy cardboard. They investigated a large box of all kinds of materials to find the clothes they wanted for their figures. They went outdoors and collected twigs, leaves, and branches. Those who wanted to depict a wheelchair out in the snow examined very carefully the wheelchairs in the classroom. They cut out material for clothes and stapled them to the figures.

Although the teacher gave the children physical help, they used their own ideas. The creation, however, would have been impossible without the participation of an adult during the whole process.

This was a creative process in which children and adults worked together, enabling the children to be artists.

The children took a particularly exciting moment in their lives and gave it permanent form. They learned a new way to relate an event, and used their abilities to perceive, to feel, to think, and finally to create their own works of art, based on their own sensory experiences. Such creation allowed the children to synthesize feelings into an integrated, imaginative whole, and to depart from the concrete.

It is unimportant whether or not a child produces a pretty picture. The importance lies in the process by which the child learns to create, and in the growth and understanding he achieves. In making a picture he gives form to an experience with which he thoroughly identifies himself; in turn, the experience itself takes on greater meaning for him. In the course of his work he handles many new and different materials, he uses new motions, and concentrates on how to recreate his experiences; the child creates a whole out of parts. This entire process adds to his ability to integrate various elements. Visual, tactile, and kinesthetic stimuli are integrated to produce the final creation.

The aim of creative activities is to give the children opportunities to express their particular experiences of the environment, to bring these into clearer focus, and to make them more understandable.

Chapter **5**

LANGUAGE DEVELOPMENT

Language development is seriously interfered with in a large percentage of children with multiple handicaps. The failure to develop adequate language may be due to long isolation, to brain damage, or to involvement of the speech mechanism. An early childhood curriculum for these children must, therefore, include an enriched language program. This may be designated as a language atmosphere plus structured language periods.

Martin Deutsch, in discussing the problem of facilitating development in the preschool child, describes a language program as follows:

A language training program would require the creation of a rich, individualized language environment, where words are repeatedly placed in a meaningful context, and where the child is allowed multiple opportunities for expressive language demonstrations as well as for receiving language stimuli under optimal conditions and being encouraged to make appropriate responses.[18]

Although he is discussing the disadvantaged child (and one who is chronologically younger than the multiply handicapped children who are the subject of this book), this description of a language

[18]"Facilitating Development in the Pre-School Child," *Merrill-Palmer Quarterly of Behavior and Development* 10, no. 3 (1964): 260.

program can be applied to the multiply handicapped child. The important point here is that one cannot expect the children automatically to learn to use language in the process of maturation— even when they are exposed to rich learning experiences in a controlled classroom environment. The experiences must be complemented with a consciousness of the role of language and a deliberate use of language in communication with the children and throughout the teaching process.

Since children learn to speak and use language as a result of their social relationships with adults, the first prerequisite to designing a language program is to delineate just how the adults will provide the atmosphere within which the children live. This atmosphere should help children to be motivated to use language to state their needs, to communicate with each other, to express their ideas, and to interpret and relate to their environment.

Teachers must be careful to use the best language of which they are capable, so they may serve as language models for the children. Good language does not mean the use of complex words, but rather simple words whose meaning the children can grasp in a context of well-constructed sentences.

Directions should be given verbally as often as possible. According to Dr. Alexandre R. Luria, "The accomplishment of a simple action on verbal instruction can be regarded as the core of voluntary behavior regulated by speech."[19]

When a child carries out an action as the result of verbal instructions, "he retains the traces of verbal instructions in his memory for a long time. Thus he learns how to formulate his own wishes and intentions independently, first in externalized and then in inner speech. He thus creates the highest forms of purposive memory and deliberate activity. What he could previously do only with adult's help, he is now able to do unassisted. This fact becomes the basic law in a child's development."[20]

The need to use language to help a child carry out tasks cannot be sufficiently stressed. The tendency, when working with multiply handicapped children, is to make little use of language for com-

[19]Alexandre R. Luria, *The Role of Speech in the Regulation of Normal and Abnormal Behavior* (New York: Liveright, 1961), p. 51.
[20]*Ibid.*, p. 17.

munication or as a tool for the development of cognition. Teachers often assume "they just won't understand."

A Language Environment

To help children develop confidence in their own ability to communicate, adults need to listen very carefully to the children's speech. Those who have problems in formulating their thoughts and expressing them in language need time to express themselves. In this respect children need the teacher's patience and understanding, not verbal help. Care should be exercised to permit children to communicate their needs in their "own language."

Many of these children understand language but cannot use it to communicate their ideas. For instance, a child might take his teacher by the hand and walk her to the door when he wants her to open it. But if his teacher tells him to wash his hands, he might go to the sink and do so. But he cannot say: "Open the door," or "I've washed my hands." It is the teacher's job to use verbal communication with the children in order to help them act in response to words. Instead of taking a child to the basin, she should tell him to go to it. When he first comes to class, he may not be able to carry out any action in response to verbal directions. Therefore, training should begin by taking a child through the motion as the teacher describes what she is doing.

For example, if a teacher asks a child to bring her a book from a shelf and the child fails to respond, he may not have understood her. So she takes the child by the hand, walks to the shelf, and gets the book. At the same time she says to the child, "Johnny, here is the shelf, here is the book." The teacher must envelop her children in language. They need to learn that sounds form words and that words bring results.

There should be a short period during the day for exploring the room and naming the objects, they see—window, door, table, wall, light, etc. There could be a brief period each day for exploring, touching, and naming.

Adults and children should engage in conversation during all free time of the day—before class begins, while walking outdoors, while preparing for lunch, and so on. During these free exchanges the children should not be corrected, even though some of their language might appear to be bizarre. These are the periods for using language without constraint.

In language training there should be a definite plan of development and purpose: to increase the children's vocabulary; to help them use language to relate to and interpret their environment; and to lay the basis for the acquisition of academic skills.

In any group of multiply handicapped young children, some will have more language skills than others. The more advanced children will help the others. Children with speech problems should be given time to formulate their thoughts and find the words they need. All questions should be treated with care. Every advance in the use of language should be greeted with praise. The child who says "Hi" for the first time has made a great step forward.

Teachers should greet the children by name each morning even though some might not respond. After many months there may be a dramatic breakthrough. For example, for months a teacher would stand near the lockers at school and greet Billy each morning as he came to kindergarten. Billy had cerebral palsy, little vision, and no speech. He never responded in any fashion. Together they hung up his coat and then would go into the classroom. One morning the teacher was busy in the classroom when Billy arrived. Suddenly she heard, "Hi—Hi—Hi." The sound come from the hall. When she went outside, there stood Billy in front of his locker, with his thumb in his mouth, calling out, "Hi—Hi—Hi." He used only that one sound for a long time but slowly began to make progress.

Naming and Classifying Objects

During the regular classroom periods, concrete objects can be presented to the children. The teacher should name the object and pass it around, giving the children time to examine it and to ask questions. The teacher also should question the children in such a fashion that she might help them arrive at their own conclusion— How does it feel? Smooth or rough? Is it as large as a book or smaller than a top?

After exploring and investigating the different properties of the objects, the children should be encouraged to describe them in their own words. The children who can speak generally describe objects in terms of their use and their likenesses and differences.

Objects grouped together on a table might include one item that does not belong in the group. For example, the teacher may put together play money, a wallet, and a shoe and ask the children to find the object that does not belong. When they find it, she should ask them to name it, describe it, and tell why it does not belong with the others. This part of the program is intended to help the children begin to abstract and classify.

Use of the Tape Recorder

Use should be made of a tape recorder to increase language awareness. The teacher should tape her own voice singing to the children and let them hear the tape. She should tape the children singing, speaking to each other, and giving the morning greeting. When the tapes are played for them, the children delight in hearing their own voices. This experience acts as a strong motivating force for experimenting with language.

There are many machines on the market that give an instant playback on a voice recording. It's worth the teacher's time to investigate these "talking machines." The children's interest is caught and held when they hear their teacher's voice, a classmate's voice, or their own voices played back to them.

The use of language to relate experiences can be facilitated by a tape recorder. For children who make use of language, a daily period can be set aside when they may dictate the story of a familiar event. They might compose stories dealing with home, the weather, a school activity, or a special event. Any experience they want to relate can be used and recorded. The teacher should play it back so that they can hear what they said, with all the mistakes in language structure and pronunciation. After a period of time, children who have been exposed to an intensive language program will hear the errors and be able to correct them.

The Use of Stories

The first stories chosen for these children should be simple and full of meaning. A skillful teacher can use stories to increase the children's vocabulary and to teach them sentence construction. In order to accomplish this goal, stories with high interest value should be chosen: action stories, stories with beauty of language, stories that either contain familiar experiences or are purely imaginative. (See the Appendix for a list of suggested story books.)

After a story has been read and thoroughly discussed, the children can dramatize it in their own words. They act as characters in the story, and the teacher narrates to give sequence to the retelling. With this approach the reading of a story further widens the experience of the children and gives them facility with language. When possible these sessions should be taped and then played back for the children to hear themselves speak. After the tape is played, the teacher should conduct a discussion to help the children evaluate their dramatization and encourage them to be self-critical.

Nonsense Rhymes and Jingles

This is one area in the language program that is not based on concrete experience. Like all the children, the multiply handicapped are enchanted with nonsense rhymes and jingles. The infectious rhythm of the nonsense rhyme is a delight. Even multiply handicapped children know that the line, "the dish ran away with the spoon," can't be true. These children do have a sense of the ridiculous and they delight in this topsy-turvy nonsense world.

Nursery Rhymes

Learning to recite nursery rhymes gives children a delight in the use of sounds. And acting out nursery rhymes gives the physically handicapped child a chance to use his body unselfconsciously. There is so much fun in the rhyme that if his motions are awkward, no one seems to care. Nursery rhymes are full of action. Sometimes a teacher first has to act out the motions, but often the children manage to figure them out for themselves.

Following are some ways in which multiply handicapped children figured out how to compensate for their handicaps in order to act out the rhymes:

Little Miss Muffet

A little girl sat on the floor pretending to eat. A boy very quickly crawled over to her and touched her. She got down on all fours and scrambled away. Neither of these children could walk. Crawling was their only independent form of locomotion.

Jack Be Nimble

A boy on Canadian crutches placed two blocks on the floor. Then, supporting himself on his crutches, he hopped over the blocks.

Almost any of the nursery rhymes lend themselves to pantomime. While the children sing or chant the verses, the teacher should read the nursery rhymes aloud. (She also should have various records of nursery rhymes with musical accompaniment.) She should try to have the children sing or chant in unison. When she judges that the children are ready, the teacher acts out the nursery rhyme. Then she picks a child to act out the rhyme. While the other children chant, one child makes the motions directed by the nursery rhyme. This is one form of following directions. It is also pantomine directed by poetry.

Uses of Poetry

"A pre-school child's own versemaking and his irresistible attraction to poetry—to hear and memorize it—serve a temporary, soon-to-pass, but very strong need for his mental growth . . . precisely at this age does poetry serve as the most powerful means of shaping the thoughts and feelings of the child, to say nothing of the way it helps him to orient himself in his language and to enrich his speech."[21]

Very few multiply handicapped children are exposed to poetry. This deprives them of that "powerful means" for growth. The cur-

[21]Chukovsky, p. 96.

riculum, therefore, should include poetry experiences of many kinds.

On the simplest level, the teacher can make use of rhymes as she helps the children through the routine of the day. For example, she might make up rhymes for washing hands. She and the individual child recite them together as she shows him how to wash his hands, pull down a paper towel, dry his hands, and let the water go down the drain.

Poems with simple rhyming words are good to read aloud, until the children are familiar with the words. Then the teacher should read the poem, pause, and have the children supply the missing, rhyming word. This can be done well with nursery rhymes.

Making up poetry is one of the creative experiences with language. Children can be encouraged to compose a poem together, with various children contributing to the thought and the words. Special poems are composed for special occasions, such as birthdays, holidays, and trips away from school.

Poems that are rich in imagery and that convey an emotion or a mood should be read aloud, and then the children asked: Whom does that make you think of? What place does this poem make you think of? Did you ever do that? In this way the poems are related to their own experience and knowledge.

The teacher can make up her own picture book of favorite poems and then record these poems on tape. When she is busy with other activities, some of the children can look at the picture book of poetry while they follow the teacher's voice on tape.

The Speech Therapist and the Teacher

It is in the use of language that the sharpest differences often manifest themselves in a group of multiply handicapped children. Regardless of such differences, all these children function far below the level of the nonhandicapped child. Handicapped children need a rich environment, and many of them will profit from individual work with a speech therapist.

The teacher is responsible for creating an environment wherein oral language dominates the scene. The language must be meaningful to the child, and he should learn how to respond to it in some fashion. The speech therapist has to work very closely with the teacher. Just as in the case of the physical therapist, the teacher must integrate the work of speech therapist into her general curriculum. Our experience has been that it is preferable to have a speech therapist in the school rather than to take a child to a clinic for therapy. Language is so related to the total school program that it seems an artificial separation to have a therapist work on language apart from the school program. If a child is being seen in a speech clinic, a visit to the school should be arranged by the therapist to see and hear the child in the school environment.

The most important phase of the language program is for the teacher to talk with or to the child. Often, because a child does not respond, adults tend to direct him physically rather than verbally, but even nonverbal children have language abilities. Perhaps their skills will develop into a verbal language in time. Regardless, a child needs to *hear* language. If only for his emotional development, it is necessary for him to feel that he is being addressed. The child who repeats a direction while he is doing the action is using language as a form of support. For example, a child might say, "Bobby put the paper in the wastebasket," repeating the direction as he performs the action. This is not simply echoing the adult. It is making use of language.

We may not always be able to measure the results of the work in the classroom. The hope of the teacher rests in the total continuous educational process, and in this process all forms of communication are vital.

Chapter **6**

CURRICULUM OF DAILY ACTIVITIES

Instead of presenting a traditional curriculum, this section suggests daily activities from which each teacher may select the activities which meet the needs of her children.

Work Periods

Some period during each day should be set aside to work with materials. Children should begin to learn the difference between work and play—that spinning a top is play, and sitting at a table with a task to complete is work. The task is a problem to be solved. It should be simple and geared to the child's ability and interest span. Unlike the normal child, the multiply handicapped child seems to function in a perpetual readiness program.

During these work periods the children should be given problems that will introduce them to different sizes and shapes. These first materials should stress likenesses and differences—matching and comparing. For these activities the teacher can use puzzles, texture boxes, color cones, nests of cups, blocks, beads, pegs and pegboards, and many of the Montessori materials.

Matching and Comparing

(1) The Texture Box

The teacher may wish to start with gross tactile experiences. She would give the child a piece of sandpaper to feel and then put before him the sandpaper, a piece of velvet, and a piece of wool and have him pick out the sandpaper by feeling all the pieces of material. After introducing him to various other textures, she would let him match pieces of the same texture by picking out pieces that feel the same.

(2) Blocks

The teacher would show the child a red block, give him four blocks of different colors, and ask him to find the red block in the group.

Matching and comparing—learning likenesses and differences—can be done by color, shape, and texture. The teacher should have a treasure chest of materials which will interest a child and help him in these first basic steps. Brightly colored puzzles of no more than three or four pieces are part of the teacher's tools.

Another simple task is copying a design of pegs on a pegboard. For this activity the teacher uses, say, a blue pegboard and red pegs. She creates a design and the child copies the design on another board.

Using a large box with slots and inserting red blocks and blue blocks alternately until one reaches the end of the row is another activity.

A board with cut-out designs for square and round pegs is another useful material. To solve this problem the child has to place a square block in the proper place then a round block in its place until he has covered the whole board.

Visual Activities

Effective use can be made of films and slides. Slides which show the children in the classroom or on an outdoor expedition are high in interest value. As the teacher shows slides of the children, she can call out the names of individual children. Or she may ask them, "Who is that child?"

The children can learn to see themselves and understand themselves better through the use of films. Perhaps once a week a teacher may set aside time to show slides or a film of the class. She may then progress to the use of filmstrips.

Activities in Daily Living

Dressing Skills

To teach a child how to manipulate a zipper, the teacher can make a small zipper bag and put a reward inside. She then demonstrates how to pull the zipper and "finds" the reward. Then she helps the child manipulate the zipper and lets him take the reward. After she has worked with the child, he will learn to pull the zipper by himself, motivated by the reward he finds in the bag.

A large doll wearing a coat with big buttons can be used to start a child manipulating buttons. The size of the buttons can be gradually decreased. To teach how to lace, the lacing shoe is still the best device.

These dressing skills can be made interesting for the children by having a regular period set aside in the morning for this kind of "work." The period should last just as long as the children's interest span allows. These activities are used primarily to reinforce the dressing skills that are taught as part of putting on and taking off clothes. The best time to teach these skills is when the children come to school, but a teacher does not always have enough time to teach each child as he arrives in the morning. She has to organize her time so that she can teach each child as much as she can when he arrives. The children can be taught to start taking off their coats while the teacher goes from one to the other, giving as much help as each one needs. Then the teacher takes each child in turn to his cubicle while her assistant stays with the group.

A child in a wheelchair who cannot take one arm out of a coat and then the other can be taught to pull his coat over his head, once the coat has been pulled up to his waist. The principle in this teaching is to give each child as much independence as possible.

Toileting

Mothers should be informed that none of the children are to come to school in diapers. If a child is not toilet trained, he should wear rubber pants. Children should be taken to the lavatory at regular intervals. For physically handicapped children the toilet should be equipped with railings so a child can push himself back and hold on to the railings once he is seated. Children should be given a reasonable amount of time to take care of their needs. They should be helped to learn how to wipe themselves, flush the toilet, and pull up their underclothing. Good performance should be rewarded with a pat on the head or words of praise.

The sinks should be adapted in various ways so that any child can learn to wash his hands. For example, children in wheelchairs should have room enough to wheel their chairs under one of the sinks. (See also the chapter on physical plant.)

Careful note should be made of each child's progress. As a child develops independence, he should be given the opportunity to take responsibility for his own needs.

Feeding

Lunch time is the time both for eating and quiet conversation. Plenty of time should be allotted for lunch.

The children should go to the sink one at a time to get washed up for lunch. While the individual child is getting washed, the group may be listening to a record or a story. But whatever the activity, it is low keyed.

Some of the children may help to set the table. It is a good idea to have individual place mats which indicate where to put down the plate, cup, and silverware. This helps the table setters know where to place things.

When all the children are washed and the table set, everyone comes to the table. The teacher, the assistant, and the aide sit with the children and help those who need to learn how to eat at a table. For children who have difficulty in holding a spoon there are various devices which can be used. Spoons with bent handles that are easier to grasp can be purchased. Some teachers have tried winding masking tape around the spoon, making it easier to grasp.

If a child has difficulty scooping up food, the teachers may give him a bowl instead of a flat plate and help him push his food to the edge of the bowl and then scoop it up.

Teachers can find many resources of suggested devices. One excellent resource for help in working with physically handicapped children is the United Cerebral Palsy Association. Resources for help in working with blind children are the Lighthouse, The American Foundation for the Blind, and The New York Institute for the Education of the Blind. One could go on listing resources, but for the most part teachers will devise many aids on their own, because so often the device must fit the needs of the particular child.

These children will take a much longer time than nonhandicapped children to learn the simple skills of daily living, but it is precisely these skills that are vital to their social development.

An Ordered Day

Multiply handicapped children need a day where events follow each other in orderly sequence. They do not easily accept changes, since they have little confidence in the environment, and changes represent a threat to them. Children gain a sense of order by knowing just what the activities of the day will be, whom they will be with, and what changes may occur. These children welcome routine because so much of their lives has been disorganized. The day's activities must include plenty of time for them to accomplish the routine, since it takes a great deal of time for them to move around.

They can be helped to grasp the sequence of events if the teacher discusses with them what they are doing today, what they did yesterday, and what they will do tomorrow. This adds to their sense of security and helps them to see relationships. When the children learn through their own experiences that the atmosphere in the school is accepting of them, and that they will not be faced with sudden drastic changes, they will gain in assurance and trust. Then they can learn how to accept change without panic.

Their tools and toys should be in order in the room where they work; it is important for them to be able to find things in their places. Materials should not be crowded together, because it is easy for these children to become confused by too many objects. A teacher should give thought to her presentation of materials. She may introduce one thing at a time. Or she may introduce a number of objects related to each other. Her specific method is based on the realization that these children must have materials presented in an orderly fashion so that they have time to digest and to assimilate their learning experience.

A creative, living curriculum is very stimulating. The activities arouse excitement, interest, and enthusiasm. These children should not haphazardly be exposed to stimuli. In order to benefit from a program which makes demands of them and introduces them to so many new experiences, they must live within a stable orderly environment.

Building a Unified Special Project

At least once during the year the teacher should select one special project. She discusses it with the children, who then make the first plans. The project should revolve around a festival or special occasion that produces high motivation. The teacher's goal is to give the children an opportunity to use all their developing skills in one effort with a definite theme and, if possible, with an end in view.

One such project could be related to Christmas. The final goal might be a party in school, to which the children invite another class. Activities for the project can be as follows: collect pine cones for table decorations; make gifts for family; design and make Christmas cards; dictate messages to go with the cards; dictate invitations to party; make invitation cards; write a playlet to perform at the party; memorize poems to recite at the party; practice songs for a community sing with the guests; and prepare simple refreshments for the party.

This type of project will help give the children a feeling for sequence and the relatedness of activities.

Creative Activities and Academic Learning

The creative, living curriculum is designed to lay the basis for academic learning. Like all learning for the multiply handicapped child, academic learning must be rooted in concrete experiences. The creative phase of the total educational program introduces the child to concrete experiences, helps him to make abstractions from them and to gain insight into relationships, and guides him toward forming concepts.

One of the major goals in educating a multiply handicapped child is to enable him to solve problems and to discover cause and effect relationships on his own. Every area of the curriculum should be designed to develop into the next stage of learning. The work periods in the classroom should be directly related to the living experiences of the child.

In exploring and interpreting the environment, the child is given innumerable opportunities to note likenesses and differences. These observations are reinforced with materials in the classroom, and the child is gradually led to match and compare.

The language program is particularly constructed to lead toward formation of concepts based on the child's own observations. Language is used to make abstractions of objects and leads toward classifying groups and setting up categories.

In active games a child learns how groups are formed and how his group can be divided in half. This concept is reinforced in the classroom with verbal games and building blocks.

The learning experiences are embedded in the creative living curriculum. One goal of the program is to develop each child's potential for the acquisition of the tools of learning.

Chapter 7

INTRODUCING THE TOOL SUBJECTS

Children do not all learn the same things at the same time, even when exposed to the same stimuli. Each child has his own tempo of development. The teacher must be sensitive to this. Timing means knowing *when* to present a certain task to a particular child. Special education is *curriculum modification*. The following activities are presented for the teacher's guidance and use. They all have been used with multiply handicapped children, to lay a groundwork for academic learning.

Recognizing Likenesses and Differences

The aim of this part of the program is to help the child bring order into his world and lay the foundation for later skills. Following is a list of materials and methods to be used by the teacher.

Size—learning to distinguish between big and small

The teacher starts with what is known, concrete, and simple to do. It is best to use an activity the child can do by himself after the teacher has introduced it.

Blocks, beads, pebbles, and disks, used with a sectioned box with removable slats

Each one of the materials has the same texture. The only difference is in size. A child is given first a box with just two sections. In one section he has to place a small block, pebble, bead, or disk; in the other section, a large one. After he has finished his work, the teacher and child check to see if it is correct. When the child has learned to discriminate between large and small, a third section, in the middle of the box, is added. Then the materials are graded in three sizes.

The box has a number of removable slats so it can be made to have many sections. With each advance a child makes, the teacher introduces smaller objects.

A large, wooden triangle with holes of graduated sizes and beads of graduated sizes

When the child has learned something about size, he can be given this device, which is a self-checking material. The holes in the triangle are of different sizes. When a child picks up a small bead and puts it in a large hole, the bead rattles around in the hole. The child is taught to feel and see if the bead really fits and to listen for a sound as he turns it in the hole. Only when the bead fits the hole exactly has he found the appropriate bead.

Montessori board of ten cylinders graded for size

A child learns to place these cylinders in the board by working gradually from the smallest to largest. Even children who have the use of only one hand can work with these materials.

Beads and string (beads of two sizes only)

The child is shown how to put two small beads and then one large bead on a string. His work for that period would be to continue with the pattern—first two small beads and then one large one. At the end of the period the teacher and child check to see if the beads have been strung correctly.

Nest of cups and color cone

These are used so that the child can discover that a small object can fit into a larger one and that there is a graduation of sizes.

All of the above "work" has certain common ingredients: (1) The material used had only one difference—size; (2) The child could do the activity independently after a period of work with his teacher; and (3) The work involved movement along with a sense of touch.

Recognition of Forms

Cylinder-shaped beads, square beads, and section box

The teacher first helps the child to discover the difference between cylinder-shaped and square beads by examining them. Then together they put the cylinder-shaped beads in one section of the box and square beads in the other section. Then the child works by himself.

Round and square beads of the same size and a board with cut-out holes to fit the shapes

This board is simple to make. It has 100 one-half-inch alternating round and square holes with matching pegs. This board can be used only by children who have use of both hands. They have to put the pegs in the board in order, straight across the top line and then down to the beginning of the second line, until all the holes are filled. They are shown how to guide themselves by keeping one finger in the hole they are to fill, while with the other hand picking up a peg to put into the hole.

The primary object of this board is to teach the children to recognize forms and to place them in the holes they fit. Beyond this the board is an excellent preparation for learning to follow a line from left to right and from top to bottom.

Form boards

The teacher starts with simple form boards that have only three pieces—a circle, a square, and a triangle. When the children learn to fit the pieces into the correct places on the first form board, they go on to boards with more forms. At first the forms are all the same size. Then the child progresses to boards where the forms are of different sizes. Thus, they learn not only to recognize forms, but also to see that the same forms can have different sizes.

Puzzles

One can make a puzzle box with sections for blocks of different shapes and sizes. Even a handicapped child who has poor use of his hands can take this box and turn it over. The child can then pick up one piece at a time and fit it into the section where it belongs. Commercial puzzles can be used, and it is best to start with the simple ones. Some have only three pieces and are easy to put together. One can progress from these to puzzles that have a number of pieces and that call for a greater degree of recognition and manipulation.

Differences in Sounds

Teaching sounds is usually suitable for group experiences. Useful materials include bells, rhythm instruments, a piano, and a clock.

Bells

One can buy bells that are all the same size but each one has a different tone and a different pitch. The children listen to each bell and then begin differentiating: they notice that one bell has a higher sound than the other. And one goal is to teach the children to ring the bells in an ascending scale.

Rhythm instruments

Here it is possible to explore and associate the different sounds and shapes of each instrument. A triangle makes a very different sound from a tambourine, sticks, or cymbals, etc.

Piano

Sound discrimination on the piano can be used for learning the nature of the scale. As the notes go up the children raise their hands, and as the notes go down the scale they lower their hands.

Clock

The ticking of the clock is used to differentiate the way the clock sounds when close to the ear from how it sounds when it is a distance away.

Recognizing likenesses and differences forms the base of all our teaching. In the classroom motor sensory training is guided and structured with the aim of creating a foundation for learning skills. Although all the children are exposed to motor sensory training, they all do not profit equally. All of them do learn however. Some children go into a program which has limited goals and emphasizes self-care and motor skills. For other children this program forms the basis for acquiring academic skills. All the children move on into programs adapted to their level of development.

Spatial Orientation

Concepts of up and down, left and right, across and over, under and on top, and top and bottom are necessary for learning to move oneself in space, to read, and to work with numbers. All of the learning situations of the entire day should contribute to helping children pick up clues for spatial orientation, another concept leading to academic skills.

Up and Down

The teacher can start by teaching the children that to reach their heads they have to put their hands up; to reach their toes they have to put their hands down. Lifting hands, as the notes of the scale are played, can help to establish the concept of up and down. Songs and games, such as "Up to the ceiling and down to the floor," are also effective.

Top and Bottom

One can make a board that has a place for one bead on the top, two beads on the next row, three beads on the third row, etc., down to the last row, which has a place for ten beads. The children can be taught to locate the top by finding the place that has only one bead, the bottom by finding the place with ten beads.

Summary

The recognition of gross likenesses and differences and the acquisition of spatial orientation are the foundation stones of later learning. To lay this foundation, we make use of sensory motor training and language. A structured work period, wherein children are given specific tasks and are taught methods of working out their particular problems, is imperative for learning. Work periods should always be adapted to the special needs of the child, both in relation to his long-term goals and in terms of his reactions on a particular day. Progress or lack of progress should be noted in the anecdotal records kept by the teachers and should be discussed by the teachers and therapists. When special problems arise, they should be discussed by the teacher and the other members of her team. Changes should be made when the staff agrees that the program is not meeting the needs of a child.

Chapter 8

ARITHMETIC

Counting

The formal part of the school day begins with the morning group. Counting can be the first activity after the morning song and the morning greetings. The teacher can begin by counting the children. A child walks or is wheeled around the circle and touches each child's head in succession. The child in the circle says "here," and the counter identifies the child and says the next number. From this beginning the children can progress to counting as they listen to the voices, without touching each child's head. Each child simply says "here," one after the other, and the child taking attendance identifies each child and counts.

Then they can go on to counting the missing children. Perhaps there are six in the group, and two are missing. The two missing children added to those present, they learn, would make the total enrollment. Then they might go on to counting the number of adults in the room. Each adult says "here" in turn. The number of adults would be added to the number of children to find the total number of people in the room. Only a few of the children may be able actually to add, but many may learn to count aloud and arrive at a total with the help of the teacher.

In addition to morning counting, throughout the day there are various opportunities for counting experiences. A child can count the steps as he goes up and down the stairs. When a child serves milk or juice in the classroom he can count the number of children and adults in the room and then count out the number of glasses that are needed. Or if a child helps to place chairs in a circle, he is told how many are needed and he can then count the chairs as he places them.

Through these experiences the teacher learns something of the children's counting concepts. The counting experiences of the day are used in order to give the children some concept of how counting is used for everyday purposes.

Introduction to Rational Counting

Materials of use in teaching rational counting include blocks, spools, coins, beads, pebbles, and a box. The problem for the child might be to put ten blocks, or spools, in the box. First, the teacher should go through the procedure. She has the child give her ten blocks, one by one, counting each one as it is given to her to put in the box. Then together the child and the teacher count the blocks to see if the total number is correct. The next step would be to have the child pick up the blocks and count them and put them into the box. Then again, teacher and child would check together to see if the number is correct.

Many children may need a great deal of help with this exercise before they understand just what they are doing. They may, for example, pick up a block and count it and then count it a second time as they put it into the box. It takes time before they understand that they are counting blocks, not just counting numbers aloud. The relationship between the block and the number is not easy for some of them to grasp, and this procedure may have to be modified in a number of ways for different children.

One method is to put a few blocks down and ask the child to give them to the teacher. After he has finished counting and has given the blocks to the teacher, she would ask, "How many did you give me?" When the child replies, then the teacher and child count the blocks together to see if the number is correct.

By introducing a number of different approaches, the teacher may be able to help the children do this work independently.

She can give them more than the number of items assigned to put in the box and tell them to stop when they have reached the number. The teacher should encourage the children to check their own work—find their mistakes, and make their own corrections. Only after they have gone through this process should they indicate that their work is finished, and then with the teacher, they can check to see if the total number is correct. Various materials, as mentioned above, should be used, so that the children learn that the number is not affected by the type of material.

Learning to Manipulate Numbers

The manipulation of numbers can be taught with the use of several materials: blocks and slip board, marbles and rubber trays, sticks glued on cards, number books with shapes in sandpaper, coins, and a plastic container.

Blocks

The teacher should start with equal groups of blocks say, two on the table and two in the slip board. She puts them together and has four blocks, takes two away and has two left. This should be varied with many different materials and methods, but always with the same aims, adding and taking away.

Marbles and rubber trays

With these materials, the children can learn to break numbers down and build them up. The trays have eight places for marbles. The problem might be to add five plus three. The child puts five marbles in one tray and three in the other and then by counting finds the answer. One can progress from this to taking the number and breaking it into smaller parts. The number might be ten, and the problem would be to break it into three parts. The child would have three rubber trays into which he could place his marbles, but they must then add up to the number ten. Or the problem might be to take the number six and break it into two equal parts.

Sticks and cards

One can make large cardboard cards with pegs to teach adding by two. There are two pegs on each side of the "problem card." The teacher can also make smaller "answer cards" with four pegs on each. The child has to find the answer first by counting, then by partial counting, and then by adding. He has to find the correct answer card and put it on the large problem card. One can progress from this stage to using a peg to represent five or ten, thus eliminating some of the counting.

Coins and plastic box

The teacher can use pennies, nickels, and dimes for this lesson. The children first learn to distinguish the coins by appearance and then by meaning—five pennies equal a nickel, two nickels equal a dime, and ten pennies equal a dime. Then a nickel is placed in the box, and a child has to put in enough pennies to equal the nickel. The same method is used for the dime, first with pennies and then two nickels.

Number books

A number book contains circles of sandpaper with the appropriate numerals printed underneath. On the first page is just one circle of sandpaper and underneath the number symbol for 1. The second page has one circle on one side and a line of raised dots leading to another circle on the other side of the page. The numeral 1 is underneath each circle, and at the bottom of the page are two circles and the number symbol 2.

The process of taking away is far more difficult to grasp than addition. The children do not master the concept of *less* as readily as they do the concept of *more*. To teach subtraction one can use the same materials used for addition, but should spend more time on the process of learning and manipulating the materials.

Number symbols and objects

Small cans with lids (those used for 35 mm film), beads, and a box are the materials needed for this teaching technique. Across the cover of the box should be five holes, and under the holes the numbers 1 through 5. Above each hole there should be a matching number of pegs. The child has to take a can, fill it with an assigned number of beads, and then place the can in the hole that matches the number of beads in the can. For example, a can with three beads would go into the hole that has the numeral 3 below it. The child could check by counting the number of pegs above the hole. For children whose hands are too involved to use cans, the teacher can provide plastic jars that have larger lids that can be screwed more easily.

At the next stage, the cans with the beads and labels are used. A child works with his teacher: he sees the number 5 and says it, then opens the can to find out whether or not he has been correct in naming the number.

As children learn to identify numbers, they use a combination of tangible materials and numerals in their answers. For example, the teacher might illustrate an addition problem with marbles. Instead of putting the marbles in a tray for the answer, the children, who would have several slips of paper with numerals, would pick out the right number slip and place it in the tray.

There are innumerable ways to present number experiences, but they should always start with tangible materials. For these children one must spend a long time with materials before introducing numerals. Then one can use a combination of tangible materials and numerals, and finally, when and if the child is ready, one can move to the use of symbols alone.

Materials for Children with Poor Use of Their Hands

Sectioned Box

A large sectioned box with removable slats, and blocks is useful. One block is put on one side of the box and another block at the other end. When the child pushes the blocks together he counts and finds he has two blocks.

Two blocks would be put into each slat, and as the child pushes the blocks to the opposite end of the box he would learn to count by twos.

Number Books and Cards

It is best for the teacher to make number books and problem cards herself, since the printed books intended for nonhandicapped children often have too much on a page for the use of the handicapped. Cards that have just one example and its answer on it are best. Or, one can make cards with just the example, so that the child either has to give the answer orally or find the numeral that represents the answer. The number books should also be very simple, with just one example or one problem on a page.

To teach sequence one can use slips of paper. The number slips are scrambled in a box. The child has to find the first number and then place the numbers in sequence on his desk.

Calendars

These are excellent materials to stimulate interest in children. There are a number of types of calendars for children on various levels.

Peg Calendar for One Week

This consists of a board with seven pegs going from left to right across the board. The child has to put square beads on the board beginning with the peg on the left, which represents Sunday, putting one on each day, until he has covered a full week with seven pegs filled. This is designed to teach days of the week and their order, number of school days, and days of the weekend.

Slip Board and Slips

The slips of paper have the names of the month, days of the week, and dates of the month. All the slips are the same length so that the children cannot use length as a clue. They make their own calendars each morning by putting the slip for the day on the top of the board, then the month, and then the date.

Cardboard Month Calendars

The teacher can make a duplicate of the monthly calendar out of cardboard. A slot on the top is for the month. The child first puts the name of the month in at the beginning of the month. Then each day he fills in the number for the date under the day of the week.

Telling Time

The teacher should begin by relating telling time to the activities of the day. Before making use of the clock, the group should discuss the schedule of a day and learn something of the day's broad divisions of morning, afternoon, evening, and night. These divisions should be taught in relation to the children's activities at particular times. For example, a child may ask: "When is morning over?" He learns that morning is over when he has lunch.

The transition to telling time comes through the use of the children's experiences and the introduction of the clock. The teacher and children investigate the numbers on the clock, and then examine the long and short hands. The teacher starts by showing them how to tell time by the hour, then the half-hour, then the quarter-hour. The children move the clock hands experimentally, and then, as understanding grows, the teacher moves the hands and the children tell the time. Each child in turn should have the opportunity to set the play clock. The teacher may say, "Set the clock for the time we go to lunch," which would mean twelve o'clock. As the children progress the teacher may say, "We started to work on our clocks at ten o'clock. We have spent ten minutes working on the clock. Now set the clock for the time it is now." Or perhaps she may say, "We go out to recess at eleven o'clock. We stay outside for a half-hour. Set the clock for the time when we come indoors." These examples would delight children because they are related to their day. They have the great value of teaching them periods of time, and time as reflected on a clock.

Chapter **9**

THE PARTIALLY SIGHTED CHILD

In many multiply handicapped children there is some visual impairment. Within the general program of exploring and interpreting the environment, these children should be encouraged to look at their surroundings and to make use of their senses of hearing, touch, and smell to aid them in interpretation of what they see.

The materials used for recognizing gross likenesses and differences mentioned before—blocks, beads, etc.—for partially sighted children should be highly colored and outlined, the foreground always clearly differentiated from the background. In working with puzzles and shapes, the children should be encouraged to look at the colors and use them as clues. If their hands are small, they should use materials which are small in size but highly colored. If they have big hands and can grasp large objects, then it is best to use large materials with bright colors. One aim is to help those who can make use of their hands to achieve some degree of eye-hand coordination.

Some of the special difficulties that are present in these children are (1) lack of eye-hand coordination; (2) inability to interpret what they see; (3) distractibility due to visual stimuli, which they cannot shut out; and (4) inability to integrate what they see. (Often they see either a mass or only the parts, but they seldom see the parts in relationship to the whole.)

Though the teacher can make use of all the materials listed in the section dealing with recognition of gross likenesses and differences, there are also some special materials for partially sighted children. For example, the teacher may use a set of three blocks that are quite large and are painted with a train, a tree, a ship. Each block has two parts—half the picture is on one half, the other part on the other half. The child makes a complete tree by putting the two parts of the block together. The only clue is the picture, but it is large and sharply defined.

The teacher can also use large pieces of dark paper for background and smaller, brightly colored, shiny pieces of paper cut in different shapes to make designs. The children have to complete the design by putting the parts together.

Some of these children can work with finger paints or paint at easels. It is helpful to frame the paper on the easel with a heavy black border so they will be able to paint within the border.

The teacher can also prepare special picture books, for which the pictures are made of felt and there is only one to a page. These are usually family picture books. One picture might be of the child, the others might be of members of his family.

Special Materials

This section will deal with the special materials designed for the use of partially sighted children. Following are brief descriptions of these materials: book stands that can be placed on a desk and be raised or lowered by the child to adjust to the level most comfortable for his vision; boards covered with felt in various dark colors; white felt numbers of different sizes ranging from fairly large to enlarged ink-print size used in books for the visually handicapped; disks that adhere to the felt; cards with large numbers and sticks, blocks, pennies, and poker chips; cards with arithmetic examples and blocks and answer cards in enlarged ink print; and blocks with numbers and pictures.

Cards with Large Number and Sticks

Put a large numeral 1 and one stick on a card, a large 2 and two sticks on another card, and so forth up to ten. After a child learns to associate the number with the stick, he is given a box of blocks.

The teacher hands him a number, and he has to take out of the box the number of blocks that corresponds to the number on the card. When the child is sufficiently familiar with the process, he works by himself. He finds on his desk a number of cards out of sequence, and his work for the morning is to put the right number of blocks on each card. Pennies or poker chips might be used so that the number is not associated with blocks only.

Felt Boards, Numbers, and Disks

Put the felt board on the stand and adjust it to the child's vision. Determine this by putting a number on the board and asking the child if he can recognize it. Then he has to match the number of disks to the number on the board. At other times the board might have a number of disks, and the child would have to find the numeral that goes with the number of disks.

Blocks with Numbers and Pictures

The blocks are a set of matching pictures and numbers. One half has a number of pictures and the other half has the matching numerals. The wrong number symbol cannot be forced to fit the picture block. If the two halves do not fit together, then the child knows he has made a mistake. This has limited use since the children need to have good coordination to put these pieces together, and the association of picture with number is not always clear to them.

Cards with Arithmetic Examples and Blocks and Answer Cards

Simple examples are written in large ink print on cards. At first the child indicates his answer with blocks. This is an intermediate stage between adding and subtracting only with blocks and doing so only with numbers. As soon as he is ready to work only with numbers, the child gets a box with small answer cards. Then he has to put the number answer on the bottom of his example. If he runs into trouble, he can always refer to the box of blocks, count them out, and then find the numeral.

Learning to Read

Learning to read is a much more difficult process than learning arithmetic. Before a child is introduced to the actual symbols of reading, there are years of preparation in other reading activities.

Reading Readiness

The earliest reading activities are included in the story hour in the classroom. Nursery rhymes, jingles, poems, stories about children, fairy tales, stories about the community—all form part of the introduction to books. Many partially sighted children enter the school program with little knowledge of even the first rhymes of childhood. All the language activities and dramatics are part of the introduction to reading. Story hour in school and listening to selected radio programs that dramatize children's classics are part of the reading experience.

These reading activities are more than an introduction to reading. For children who cannot learn to read but who are intelligent, they provide a means of learning about books by hearing. Learning to gain knowledge through listening requires a different kind of training, but it is just as complex as the training for sighted children who can learn to read.

Methods

Reading activities for partially sighted children are described below. Materials for these techniques include: adjustable wooden stands, felt boards, and letters; large ink-print alphabet blocks; picture books with large ink-print labels; slips with enlarged ink-print labels; slips with enlarged ink print and small bulletin boards; and enlarged ink-print books.

Felt board and letters, alphabet blocks with large ink print

One can start teaching letter by letter. Often a child cannot "see" a whole word. The whole word is confusing, so the teacher should introduce the word letter by letter. She starts with a child's name.

First she prints the first name, naming the letters as she spells out the name. The child puts the letters, which are made of white felt, on the felt board, which is made of dark green felt. When the name is complete, he may go over it letter by letter, pointing to and saying each letter. When he is all finished he will move his head from side to side to take in the whole configuration of his name.

Alphabet blocks with large ink print can also be used. The teacher forms the name with the blocks, and the child copies the name with another set of blocks.

Picture books with large ink-print labels

Collect pictures of fruits and vegetables. Put one picture on a page and underneath each a large, ink-print label. Prepare a duplicate set of labels. The pictures of the fruits and vegetables should be highly colored so that they stand out from the background of the page. The child matches the labels in ink print with the labels in the book.

Slips with enlarged ink print and small bulletin boards

Make ink-print labels of the children's names. Then attach one name to a small bulletin board that can fit on a child's desk. The child has to find the same name in the box with the ink-print labels. All the labels should be printed in large letters.

Pre-primers

When a child has built up a reading recognition of a number of words, make books in which these words are used. The first book would contain only the child's first and last names, his address, and telephone number. From there the teacher progresses to books with the names of family members, the names of schoolmates, and a few very simple sentences in which the child's name appears.

Learning to Write

Materials for teaching partially sighted children to write include: small shapes of the square, circle, and triangle; heavy lead pencils; tracing paper; and paper with wide-spaced, clearly marked lines.

The writing system is broken down into the three basic shapes, which are illustrated with pieces of cardboard cut to square, circle, and triangle shapes. Tape a big sheet of paper to each child's desk. Then paste the shapes to the paper and help them trace the outlines of the shapes. The aim of this procedure is simply to give the children practice in holding a pencil and making it move at their direction. Often the pencil may go off the paper or out of control. These practice periods always should be kept relatively short, since they are hard on a child who is straining to control his hands.

The next step would be to make tracings with a heavy lead pencil, put them under the paper, and let the child trace over the outlines. Then pick up the tracing paper and let the child see what he had done. After this he may progress to making straight lines from top to bottom within the lines on the paper. Finally, using the basic shapes for printing, teach the child how to print the letters of his name.

This method of teaching writing can be used with children who have a problem in controlling their hands. They learn through drill and enjoy tracing forms. The reward lies in their delight when they see the shapes they have traced.

Chapter 10

THE BLIND CHILD

Mention has been made that among the multiply handicapped, one finds the blind child, and that within a program for the multiply handicapped, provision can be made for him. Although he requires a special teaching skill, this child need not be segregated because of blindness. The curriculum for the multiply handicapped, with its emphasis on sensory stimulation and spatial orientation, meets the needs of the blind child. The special skill is needed for the introduction of the child to braille. Following are some methods to use with the blind child.

Introduction to Braille Symbols

The teacher begins using braille symbols when she judges a child to be ready mentally and to have achieved some control of his hands and discrimination in the use of his hands. This readiness implies a great deal. The chronological age at which children begin to use the braille symbols varies. One child may be ready when he is six years old, while another may not be ready until much later. The reasons for this vary. Some children are so disturbed that they simply cannot concentrate long enough. Some have so little understanding of spoken words that teaching them written words would be a complete waste of time. Others have so little understanding of their general environment that they first must learn something about reality, before being introduced to words that represent experiences. Other children, who have difficulty comprehending likenesses and differences, require an extended time to learn to distinguish shapes and forms. Still others may not have the physical coordination or the tactile discrimination that are necessary to master braille. Thus, the emphasis should be on timing in determining when to introduce a child to the braille system.

Braille is a system of reading for the blind based on raised dots. The entire alphabet is formed by six raised dots. Letters are based on the number of dots and their position in space and in relationship to each other. Therefore, to be able to distinguish letters and words in braille, the child must be able to perceive with his hands the entire configuration of small dots and their relationship to the next series of dots. To be able to read braille it is necessary to have fine tactile discrimination, good hand movement, the ability to perceive form, knowledge of left and right, and the ability to perceive relationships in space. Also the reader must be able to synthesize the dots into a meaningful whole and to hold a thought suspended until the end of a sentence, since braille is read word by word.

Teaching braille to the multiply handicapped blind child calls for many adaptations. The teacher must, of course, know braille before she can teach it. Following are some special methods for the teacher who may find a blind child in her class of multiply handicapped children. Sometimes it may be possible to have a special braille teacher work with a child on a one-to-one basis, when both the classroom teacher and the braille teacher feel the child is ready for the introduction to braille materials. Nevertheless, the blind child participates with the group in all activities, except during his braille instruction. This again calls for close working together on the part of the classroom teacher and the braille teacher.

Materials

The first materials are designed to introduce the child to the braille pattern:

1. Wooden cells with six sections and marbles, models in wood with the braille alphabet, rubber braille cells with six sections and marbles.
2. Alphabet blocks made of nail heads, and a board into which the blocks can fit. (The nail heads are of three sizes, going from large to small.)
3. Metal pegs, and wooden board with small holes in six sections.
4. Two rows of cells, thumbtacks, and a small bulletin board that can fit on a desk.
5. Cards with large plaster of Paris dots in large braille symbols.
6. Braille slips and slip board.

Methods

One can use a number of methods concurrently. The aim of the early program is to introduce the child to the braille pattern and to teach him the concept of the pattern relationship.

Wooden Cells and Marbles

As an introductory device, there are many ways of utilizing the blocks (or cells). Some children respond to one method, others to a different form of introduction. Each child has a chance to explore the wooden block. He is then given a model block with letter patterns in marbles, which he is to copy using marbles. Some children learn by the use of numbers. They learn that the six holes in the block have a definite number sequence. They learn to form letters by noting that place number one is an *a*, and that by filling places one and two, a *b* is formed. Most children copy patterns and learn number sequence as they copy. Each wooden block has a nailhead on the top so that the child can find the top by touch. Give the child a slip of paper on which his name is written in braille. One does not expect the child to be able to distinguish his name, but this is one means of motivating him. He learns why he is working with the braille cells and discovers what his whole name feels like. Then the teacher begins to form the letters with the braille blocks to make a name.

Drill on letters of the alphabet is the next step. As a child learns to form his name he will ask, "How do you make a *p?*" or "Can you show me how to make a *y?*" As all children do, he will ask for help in spelling words that interest him. On the basis of his own name and the names of the other children, he learns to form all the letters of the alphabet. After he has mastered some part of forming the letters with direction from the teacher, he should be given the wooden models to work independently at forming words and names. When he has a problem in remembering how to form a letter, he refers to the model and copies the form from the model.

Every chair and desk should have the child's name on a braille slip. The teacher makes the labels, but the children help to put them on the desks and chairs. Some learn to distinguish one name from another by identifying the length of the name. Others are able to distinguish names by identifying the first letter in the name. Also, labels should be attached to the door, shelves, windows, and other features of the room. This helps the children relate the words to objects.

Rubber Cells and Marbles

The principle and the method for this activity are the same as described above. The teacher simply varies the material she works with so the children will be able to distinguish the braille pattern against a number of backgrounds for the marbles.

Metal Pegs and Wooden Board

This method was used for a retarded, multiply handicapped blind child. The cells on the board were much smaller than the wooden cells. The pegs were, of course, sharper than the marbles. Though she was retarded and had use of only one hand, that use was excellent. With her good hand, she could place the small metal pegs in the cells and then distinguish the whole pattern. She needed the extra sharpness of the pegs to be able to distinguish the beginning pattern; by placing the symbols close to each other, which was possible with a small board, she was able to find the letters and their relationship to each other.

Nailhead Alphabet Blocks

All introductory materials are designed to help a child learn by doing, that is, he has to make the symbols himself. The alphabet blocks are all made with nailheads on the top to help the child find the top by touch. Then the actual letters are made with nailheads. Thus, with these blocks, the children learn to distinguish the whole pattern by feeling the configuration of the nailheads. These blocks can be placed in a board in which the children are to form the entire alphabet by placing the letters in order. The nailheads are of different sizes; as soon as a child has mastered one size, he is given the next smaller size to work with. The smallest block size is very close to the actual size of the braille dot on paper.

Thumbtacks and Bulletin Board

Small thumbtacks are placed on the board to form names and words. The teacher guides the child's hand across the words formed by the thumbtacks. This is useful primarily for those children who cannot control their hands and would knock the marbles or blocks over before they could feel them. For some children it has no use, because they would become interested in pulling out the tacks. Materials should be chosen to meet the needs of each child.

Cards with Large, Plaster of Paris Dots Forming Braille Symbols

These are used in the same way as the nailhead blocks. But again it is a different material, and the dots are exaggerated so that a child beginning to learn the symbols can feel the difference between the card and the dot.

Alphabet Blocks Covered with Plastic Symbols

On these blocks the symbols are the size of the actual braille symbols used in books. But the material used to make these symbols is plastic, which is easier to distinguish than paper; the dots are more clearly defined in plastic.

Braille Slips and Board

Whole words are formed on braille paper. As they work with the braille blocks and other materials, the children also are given braille slips with their own names on them. When they can distinguish their own names, they get a box of braille slips and have to find their own names.

Matching and Comparing

In order to teach blind children to match and compare, the following materials may be used: two- by three-inch cardboard cards with plaster of Paris braille symbols (The symbols are in graded form; they start large, and the last ones are the size of regular braille symbols.); and slip boards and slips, with upper left-hand corner cut off box.

Symbols

The cardboard cards are used to find likenesses and differences between symbols, matching and comparing at this level before teaching the children to identify letters in braille.

A large slip board with five rows is used, and a card with a different symbol is placed on each row. The children have to find among the rest of the cards those that match and put them in the correct rows. Or a row of braille cards may be put on the board. All the cards would be the same but one, and the children have to find and take out the one that does not match.

Words

On a slip board are placed a number of words in braille. In a box is a group of slips, from which the child has to find the words that match those on the board. Another procedure is to prepare slips with words that begin with the same letter but that have different sounds, and put them in a box. The child has to separate the word according to sounds.

Slips may also be placed in a box of "whole families," and the child has to indicate the words that belong together. For example, the box might contain the words, *sing, thing, ring, king,* etc., as well as *sand, band, hand, land,* etc. It is especially important for them to recognize such comparisons, because these "family" sounds are contracted in braille. There are special symbols, for example, that represent *ing* and *and.*

Slips of staff members' names may be placed in a box for another lesson. These contain *Mr., Mrs.,* and *Miss* and make use of capital letters and periods. The child has to find two slips that match. He works with one slip board and two boxes, taking out one name, then looking for its matching slip, and discarding slips which do not match.

Building a Reading Vocabulary

The beginning words are based on the child's speaking vocabulary and experiences. The ordinary pre-primers will not be helpful since most of them are based on visual clues. These books have been written for children with sight, and the sentences have meaning with reference to pictures, which are in the ink-print book. First books for blind children should be based on familiar experiences and words. For example, one may make a first book about Christmas. Pictures, made out of felt, may be of snow, Santa Claus, trees, and the words should identify the pictures on the appropriate pages.

This kind of introductory book, however, has limited value since the three-dimensional felt "pictures" may be too distracting and since they do not give an adequate idea of their relationship to the new words. As a beginning for motivation it is good, but it is best to expose the children to experiences that widen their first-hand knowledge of letters and words, and then introduce a book made up of words only.

Filing and Classifying Words

A cardboard box is sectioned off to provide one section for each letter of the alphabet. Each section contains one word beginning with the letter for that section. The child is given a group of words in braille, and has to file each word in the appropriate section. Once he is familiar with the alphabetical sections, the words that served to guide him are removed. Before attempting this activity, the child must have many experiences in putting words beginning with the same letter on different rows of a slip board.

Chapter 11

SUMMARY

Each teacher can develop her own creative, living curriculum. The curriculum in this book is offered as an illustration of an approach to the education of multiply handicapped children. It is based on the concept that the severely handicapped child needs the same experiences as the normal child, and that these experiences can be made available to him through the planning of the teacher.

Children who are beyond the chronological age of early childhood, and alienated from the environment, are introduced to a new world of childhood. The curriculum makes it possible for them to explore and interpret the environment by having direct contact with their physical surroundings. They are encouraged to investigate with their bodies and all their senses. Through structured play they experience space, play games with other children, and act out their anxieties and fears in settings designed to enhance their life experiences.

The heart of the curriculum is a rich program of creative activities. Music includes singing, playing rhythm instruments, dancing, and listening to music of all kinds. The art program seeks to find the medium most suitable for each child and to give each one a means for expressing his concept of reality. The crafts program makes use of both conventional and unconventional materials to produce objects for use and for gift giving. The enriched language program provides for a language atmosphere, structured periods for teaching language, and the introduction to the beauty of poetry and prose.

The daily activities are designed to develop self-help skills and to introduce readiness materials for acquiring academic skills. The entire curriculum rests on an ordered day, in which the children are provided with a stable environment.

The teacher is the central figure in this curriculum. The implementation rests with her; she is the one who adapts, stimulates, and creates the program. She directs all her attention to helping the children make independent efforts in their education. Her guidance and confidence stimulate the children to engage in all the activities.

The goal of this curriculum is to provide opportunities for the development of the multiply handicapped child. The applied concept substitutes *education* for *training.*

Many multiply handicapped children exposed to this curriculum will not grow beyond the stage of early childhood in their abilities, but at least they will have grown to the limit of their potential. And some children, having lived through the rich and stimulating childhood made possible by this approach, will be able to go on to the next phase of their development, having acquired inner strength and resources. All the children will have been helped toward a measure of self-understanding and acceptance.

The curriculum includes methods and materials for introducing the tool subjects to multiply handicapped children. But no arbitrary limits are set on a child's potential for growth. The opportunities and guidance for further development are included in the curriculum.

The goal of the curriculum is to help the children *want* to learn, so they will use all their own resources for growth and fulfillment.

APPENDIX

AND

BIBLIOGRAPHY

APPENDIX

The purpose of this Appendix is to give the reader practical information and illustrations to support the material contained in the main body of the book. The Appendix contains the following:

1. The organization of a trip and suggested outings and trips to cultural centers for children.
2. A special section on games, arts, and crafts.
3. Books, materials, and equipment.
4. Example of a daily schedule.

The Appendix also contains lists of resources where teachers may find material to adapt for use with their own groups.

Organization of a Trip

Visit the place before taking the children. Determine the following:

Are there any steps?
How close are the toilet facilities?
Can wheelchairs be pushed in the area?
Can the area be explored by children on crutches?
For an all-day trip: Are there facilities where the
    children can eat lunch?

> For an outdoor outing: Is there a place for the children
> to take shelter in case of rain or thunderstorm?

If the projected trip is a visit to a museum or children's zoo, contact the education department in order to ask for special consideration since the children are blind, crippled, or otherwise handicapped. Ask if materials for the children to handle are available.

Make arrangements for the use of a bus or other means of transportation. Notify the place you are going to visit of the date and time of arrival, and arrange for any special bus permits needed for entrance. If tickets are necessary (for rides in an amusement park, admission to a theater, etc.), have them mailed to you early or arrange to have them ready for you on arrival.

Notify parents of the date and time of the trip and of anything the children may need to bring along. Arrange to have lunches sent from home or prepared in school, and see that any necessary medication is taken.

Pack extra clothes in case of accidents. Also, take along tissues and paper towels, blankets, extra sweaters, and a first aid kit.

Discuss the trip with the children; see that they know the purpose of the trip and what activities to expect.

Arrange for a sufficient number of adults, either staff members or parents, to go along so that each child is adequately supervised at all times. See that each adult knows ahead of time what his or her responsibilities are, and assign each to specific children.

Arrange seating in the bus so that children with behavior problems or special fears are closely supervised by someone who can help them feel relaxed and secure.

Upon arrival at the destination, see that all the arrangements have been made before letting the children leave the bus. Unless the bus driver is to stay with the group, agree on an exact time and place for him to pick up the children for the return trip.

Trip Suggestions

Cook-out in a park
Swimming at a pool, lake, or beach
Amusement park

Ride on a ferryboat or dayliner
A botanical garden, arboretum, or large greenhouse.
Children's zoo
Outing to see a department store Santa Claus
Natural history museum or art museum
Children's theater
Local historical society
Concert

Sources of Ideas for Trips

New York Public Library, Children's Section—books on trips for
    children.
Museum of the City of New York—publications on trips for chil-
    dren.
The Wonderful World for Children — Explorer's Guide, 1 Orchard
    Parkway, White Plains, N. Y.
New York Times—"Events for Children" section appear on Fri-
    days.

Games, Arts and Crafts

Active Outdoor Games

Racing: Children in wheelchairs sit facing each other, some distance apart, while children who are ambulatory start out together,
running from one row of wheelchairs to the row on the opposite
side of the room. If the children are blind, the shouts of children
on the side to which they are running give clues as to direction.

Hide and Go Seek: A child in a wheelchair might be "It." All the
other children hide behind trees, walls, etc. Those with visual or
orthopedic handicaps or with problems in spatial orientation may
need adult help in order to hide in an appropriate place. The child
who is "It" moves in his wheelchair to find the children. An adult
may have to push him, in which case the child would give directions

as to which way to go and when to stop. One child is sought at a time. The child who is being sought calls out, "Here," at intervals until he is found.

Ball Relay: Children form two teams, each in a line. Children who can walk are interspersed along each line with those in wheelchairs. On signal, the child at the front of each line passes the ball back, over his head, to the next child. The ball is passed until it gets to the end of the line. When the last child gets the ball, he hurries to the front of the line and starts the ball back again. This is continued until the child originally at the front of the line gets back to his place. The team whose leader returns to the front first wins. This game needs the help of more than one adult. Children in wheelchairs have to be pushed to the front of the line when it is their turn, and others need help in grasping and passing the ball. The game should be played on the grass, so that children who have poor balance will not hurt themselves if they fall. The ball should be large enough to grasp easily. A ball with a bell inside will be of help to blind children. Children with partial vision, hearing losses, or perceptual problems will be helped if the ball is a striking color.

Scatter: This game can be played inside or outside. All the children who can crawl in any way get down on their hands and knees. The teacher blows a whistle, which means "Scatter!" The children go off in any direction, and the second time the whistle blows, they stop wherever they are. The teacher throws a ball containing a bell into the center of the group. The whistle is blown a third time, and the children crawl as rapidly as possible toward the ball, as it bounces and rolls. The sound of the bell helps them locate it. The child who picks up the ball first wins the game.

Wall Target: This is a simple game in which the children throw a ball against a wall. Every child throws from a position close enough to insure that he will hit the wall. Some may stand or sit no more than a foot away from the wall, while others may be ten to fifteen feet away. This may be played by one child alone or by several children. It is not a competitive game; there is no scoring.

Teacher Ball: Children are in a row or a circle. The teacher plays "Catch" with each child in turn. She throws or may merely drop the ball into the child's hands or lap. Then the child throws it back. This is a good game for children's first experience with ball throwing. It is not a group game as such, because it allows the teacher to show each child how to catch and throw. And there are no penalties for lack of skill in this game.

Active Indoor Games

Beanbag and Bell: Attach a bell to a strap and hang it across the opening of a large wastebasket. Each child takes a turn throwing the beanbag into the basket, and the bell rings if he is successful. Ambulatory children may stand for this game, and those in wheelchairs sit. The distance of the basket from the child varies according to his skill. Blind children are directed where to throw the beanbag by the teacher, who stands directly over the basket and calls, "Here."

Ring Toss: Adaptations are similar to the above game. Instead of a bell, the sound of the ring as it hits the metal base indicates success. The game can be played on a table for children who cannot really throw, so that they can more easily see or feel where the rings land. No scoring is made until the children have developed some throwing skills.

Skillball: This is a commercial game, which can be used successfully for children with a variety of handicaps. The game has a metal base about two feet square. Light, brightly colored balls, about the size of Ping-Pong balls, are rolled up an incline to the center of the base. The object of the game is to get the balls to roll into holes that run into little "alleys" at the side. Ten, twenty, or thirty points are made if the ball rolls into one of the three holes in the board. The game can be played at a table or on the floor. Children who cannot roll a ball hard enough to get it up the incline may drop it from above the game. This can be played by one to four children.

Bowling: Equipment for this game consists of light plastic bowling pins, about a foot high. Each pin has a bell inside. Ten pins are lined up in a group, and a plastic ball, about five inches in diameter, is rolled to knock them over. A heavier ball, without much bounce to it, should be used for children who cannot roll the ball with any degree of strength. Each child counts the number of pins he has knocked over, or the game can be played without keeping score. The bells help the children to know when they have hit the pins.

Darts: A large standard target is placed on the wall. The children throw suction-cup darts at the target and get whatever score is marked in the place where the dart sticks. To help blind children aim, the teacher may either call out from near the target or tap it with a pointer. If children have difficulty in throwing to the wall, the target may be placed on the floor.

Out-to-Ten Ball: This is a version of "Hot Potato." It is played, indoors or outdoors, in a circle and can be very active. The group sits close together, and as the teacher or a child starts counting slowly, the ball is passed around the circle. The child who is holding the ball at the count of ten is out of the game. The object is to pass the ball as fast as possible so that one does not have it when the counting stops. The children move closer together to fill the gaps as some drop out and repeat the counting. They are eliminated from the game one by one until only the last child, the winner, remains. The teacher or another adult may have to help some children to reach and grasp the ball and then to pass it to the next person. In another version, the ball can be passed while a piano or record is played. The child who has the ball when the music stops is "out."

Catch the Changer: In this game one child goes away from the group while the others choose a leader. He is to make various changing sounds or motions which the others must follow. When "It" comes back, he is to guess who is guiding the group in making the changes.

Treasure Hunt: The teacher hides an object in the room, and the children hunt for it. They may walk, go in wheelchairs, walk on crutches, or crawl around the room. The only hint they are given is that it is in the room and is something familiar to them. This game really encourages exploring, because the children may go throughout the entire room. Any familiar object may be the "treasure."

Find the Block: This is a group game. One child leaves the room, while the others decide where to hide a block, a toy animal, or any other familiar toy. Then "It" comes into the room and tries to find the toy. As he goes around the room, the children give him hints by saying "hot" or "cold" to indicate whether he is near or far from the toy. If any of the children are blind, the teacher will have to tell them where "It" is going—"Now she is by the big chair . . . Now she is under the table," etc.

Circle Games and Guessing Games

"Who Is Knocking at My Garden Gate?" The children sit in a circle, with the child who is "It" in the middle. He is blindfolded or closes his eyes. Another child knocks on "Its" chair or wheelchair. "It" asks, "Who is knocking at my Garden Gate?" The child answers in a disguised voice, "I am." "It" guesses who that child is. When it becomes too easy for the children to identify each others' voices, the game may be changed so that "It" guesses by shaking hands with the child or by touching his face.

Alphabet Trip: One child begins by saying, "I am going on a trip and I am taking an apple." The next child might say, "I am going on a trip and I am taking an apple and a bell." The third child could say, "I am going on a trip and I am taking an apple, a bell, and a cap." Each child must repeat everything said by the previous child and add one more thing, which begins with the next letter of the alphabet.Whoever does not remember the whole sequence and what comes next is out of the game. The winner is the child who is left at the end. Whenever this game is played with children having many handicaps, and when it is first introduced, the teacher should help the children who cannot think of things to add to the list. Then the children can have fun without competition.

Who's Missing?   The children sit in a circle and "It" leaves the room. When "It" is gone, one child is chosen to leave the circle and place himself out of sight. "It" is called back to figure out who is missing. This game is good for children just getting acquainted with each other.

Singing Games

Singing games can range from simple finger plays to complicated acting out and dancing. Almost any nursery rhyme may be used; counting games are also good. These games can be played both outside and indoors, at school or on trips. They may be sung with or without musical accompaniment. The piano is the instrument most adaptable to these games. The teacher may also use recorded music if she wishes to give the children individual help during the singing game. A harmonica or accordion can be taken outside or on trips and helps the children feel that they can take their music wherever they go. Following are examples of several kinds of singing games that can be adapted for multiply handicapped children.

"I've Been to London"

Purpose: To have the children move to the rhythm of the song in whatever manner or pace that they can. At the same time, they use their imaginations to pretend that they are going to some part of the world, of which they may have heard.

Tune: "Turn the Glasses Over," a sea chantey.
Words: I've been to London.
         I've been to Dover.
         I've traveled this wide world all over,
         Over, over, three times over.
         Drink all the brandywine
         And turn the glasses over.

Action: During the music the children may walk, use their crutches, propel their wheelchairs, or crawl on the floor. They begin "traveling" and singing when the music starts and they stop when it does. This activity can be repeated, the children choosing different destinations each time.

"Where, Oh Where"

Purpose: To have assigned parts in singing, to sing about individual children, and to locate them by voice.
Tune: "Paw Paw Patch," a folk song.
Words: Where, oh where, is dear little (Patty)?
         Where, oh where, is dear little (Patty)?
         Where, oh where, is dear little (Patty)?
         Way out yonder in the (hallway) now.

Action: Children are in a circle. One child goes, or is taken, to another part of the room or to a room nearby. The children in the circle sing the first three lines. The child who is hiding sings the answer. Other hiding places should be used for variety. When the child returns to the circle, he chooses the next child to go out and the game continues.

"Looby Lou"

Purpose: Identification and use of various parts of the body; identifying right and left on oneself; and following directions for physical movements.
Tune: "Looby Lou," a traditional children's
         singing game.

Words: Words to the traditional song are
used without change.
Action: Children are in a circle. If they are physically handicapped, they may be seated. If only one child cannot walk, he may
have his wheelchair pushed around in the circle while the others
walk to the rhythm of "Here we go Looby Lou." If more than one
can't walk, the children may move their hands and feet forward
either from a standing or sitting position. When they come to the
words "And turn myself around," they may describe a circle with
one hand or, perhaps, another child may turn a child seated in a
wheelchair around.

"There Was a Boy"

Purpose: Enjoyment of hearing one's name in song; and to help
children get acquainted with each other.
Tune: "Bingo," a children's folk song.
Words: There was a (boy) (girl) who came to school
And (Ricky) was (his) (her) name, oh!
R - I - CKY
R - I - CKY
R - I - CKY
And (Ricky) was (his) (her) name, oh!
Action: This can be played without action, or the child named
in the song can come to the middle of the circle while the others
are singing.

Arts and Crafts Projects

Suggested Gifts that Are Simple to Make

Jewelry box	Bracelet
Leather wallet	Hot plate
Belt	Plate made of tile
Wooden lamp	Necklace
Earrings	Book ends

All the materials for making these gifts can be bought ready-to-
finish in handicraft departments or at special stores. It takes only

a few simple movements to put the objects together.

Necklace and earrings: The parts consist of stones and a chain. To make a necklace, simply paste the stones into the chain backing. Earrings are made in the same fashion.

Book ends: All that is needed is four pieces of wood of the same size. The wood is sanded and shellacked, and the pieces glued together to form the book ends.

Hot plate: Children who have learned to string beads can make this gift. Wooden sticks with holes, and beads are alternately strung together with elastic. The sticks form the hot plate.

Leather wallet: Two prepared pieces of the wallet are sewn together with a needle and leather lacing. Children who have learned how to lace can do this.

Cards for Any Occasion

Colored construction paper can be folded in half. Children choose what they want to put on the cards from boxes that may contain materials such as: shells, sequins, figures made of felt, bits of lace, small beads, etc. These give the cards a three-dimensional effect. The children glue the materials on in their own designs.

Materials for Arts and Crafts

Arts:

> Conventional materials: paint, clay, crayons, paste, brushes, easels, finger paints, paper of all kinds, cardboard, scissors.
>
> Additional materials: felt, cotton, rug scraps, lace, silk, tweed, wool, rayon, chenille, ribbons, sandpaper, twigs, branches, pine cones, logs, leaves, berries, bark of trees, ferns, popcorn, seeds, chicken wire, pipe cleaners, tin foil, sawdust, soapsuds, noodles, clothespins, aluminum foil, paper plates, feathers, sea shells, beads, sequins, tinsel.

Crafts:

> Materials: Boxes, candles, sticks of wood, leather, tile, sca-
> rabs, plastic molds, beads, wire, shells, pin backs, ear-
> ring backs, lace, wood, grout, shellac, tin cans, raffia,
> coat hangers, bottles.
> Tools: Carpenter's bench and tools (hammers, saws, screw-
> drivers, brace and bits, nails, clamps); also: scissors,
> knitting needles, brayers, stylus, lacing needles, egg
> beater, stapler.

Books, Materials, and Equipment

Storybooks

Following are suggestions for some books for the teacher to use
when she reads aloud to the children. These are all collections of
stories of daily activities, families, animals, the seasons, humor,
holidays, folk tales, fairy tales, and make-believe.

Andersen, Hans Christian. *Fairy Tales and Legends.* New York:
   Macmillan, 1935.
Association for Childhood Education International. *Told Under the
   Green Umbrella.* New York: Macmillan, 1955. Kindergar-
   ten to primary level.
———. *Told Under the Magic Umbrella.* New York: Macmillan,
   1955. Primary level.
Child Study Association of America. *Read to Me Story Books.*
   New York: Crowell, 1948. For two- to seven-year-olds.
Gagliardo, Ruth. *Let's Read Aloud.* New York: National Recrea-
   tion Association.
Kipling, Rudyard. *Just So Stories.* Compiled by J. M. Gleeson.
   New York: Doubleday, 1912.
Mitchell, Lucy Sprague. *Here and Now Story Book.* New York: E.
   P. Dutton, 1948. For two- to seven-year-olds.
Rackham, Arthur, comp. *The Arthur Rackham Fairy Book.* New
   York: Lippincott, 1950.

There are a number of excellent authors of books for young
children. They have each written several books, many of which

have become classics. These authors are listed below with mention of one of their books or the type of book they write:

Bemelmens, Ludwig: "Madelaine" stories
Beskov, Elsa: "Pelle" stories
Brown, Margaret Wise: "Noisy books"
Burton, Virginia Lee; *Katy and the Big Snow*
Gag, Wanda: *Millions of Cats*
Hader, Berta and Elmer: *The Big Snow*
Lenski, Lois: *The Little House*
McCloskey, Robert: *Make Way for Ducklings*
Milne, A. A.: Winnie the Pooh books
Petersham, Maud and Miska: *Poppy Seed Cakes*
Potter, Beatrix: *The Tale of Peter Rabbit*
Rey, H. A.: *Curious George*
Tresselt, Alvin R.: *White Snow, Bright Snow*

Rhymes and Poetry

Association for Childhood Education International. *Sung Under the Silver Umbrella.* New York: Macmillan, 1935.

Baldwin, Michael. *Poems by Children.* London: Routledge and Kegan Paul, 1962.

Benet, William Rose. *Mother Goose.* Garden City, N.Y.: Heritage Press, 1943.

Brewton, Sara W., and Edmund, John. *Sing a Song of Seasons.* New York: Macmillan, 1955.

Coatsworth, Elizabeth J. *The Children Come Running.* New York: Golden Press, 1960. Poems and stories about children of many lands.

DeAngeli, Marguerite. *Book of Nursery and Mother Goose Rhymes.* New York: Doubleday, 1954.

Field, Rachel. *Taxis and Toadstools.* New York: Doubleday, 1926.

Grayson, Marion. *Let's Do Finger-plays.* New York: National Recreation Association.

Harrington, Mildred P. *Ring Around.* New York: Macmillan, 1930.

Hubbard, Alice and Battitt, A. *The Golden Flute.* New York: John Day, 1932.

McEwan, Catherine S. *Away We Go.* New York: Crowell, 1956.

McGinley, Phyllis. *All Around the Town*. New York: Lippincott, 1948.

Milne, A. A. *When We Were Very Young*. New York: E. P. Dutton, 1924.

Segal, Edith. *Come Walk with Me*. New York: Sylvan Press, 1953.

Stevenson, Robert Louis. *A Child's Garden of Verses*. New York: Scribner's, 1905.

Thompson, Blanche J. *Silver Pennies*. New York: Macmillan, 1925.

Untermeyer, Louis. *Golden Treasury of Poetry*. New York: Golden Press, 1959.

———. *This Singing World*. New York: Harcourt, 1923.

Materials and Equipment

Materials and equipment are listed here according to the appropriate activity or function.

(1) Gross Motor Skills

a. large balls
b. skates, bicycles
c. gym mats
d. ladder boxes
e. blocks
f. trampolines
g. workbenches with hammers, saws
h. climbing stairs
i. slides
j. barrels

(2) Fine Motor Skills

a. toy clock
b. knock-out benches
c. graded circles, squares, etc.
d. construction blocks, block accessories (trains, cars, trucks, boats, planes, colored cubes, small figures of people and animals)

e. puzzles
f. crayons, paints, clay, scissors, paste, chalk
g. stacking toys
h. peg boards
i. lotto, dominoes
j. lacing shoe

(3) Sensory Development
   a. rough and smooth letters and number cards
   b. musical instruments (drums — large and small— tambourines, cymbals, triangles, various bells, sticks, maracas, sand blocks)
   c. record players
   d. tape recorders
   e. different grades of sandpaper squares
   f. flannel boards
   g. sandboxes, water tables
   h. texture box

(4) Perceptual Development
   a. hand and full-length mirrors
   b. tether balls
   c. projector
   d. color charts, templates
   e. balancing boards

(5) Play Materials and Supplies
   a. dolls, doll houses, unbreakable dishes
   b. telephones
   c. trucks, cars
   d. large picture books, magazines, mounted pictures
   e. egg beaters, varied bowls
   f. pots, pans, dishes
   g. iron
   h. washable rubber dolls

(6) Furniture
    a. sturdy tables, chairs, and desks
    b. easels
    c. cabinets
    d. cots or mats
    e. folding screens, room dividers

(7) Science Materials
    a. batteries, bells, pulleys
    b. magnets
    c. fish bowl

(8) Outdoor Accessories
    a. balls
    b. pump for balls
    c. sandbox equipment (pails, shovels, etc.)
    d. galvanized tub

A Daily Schedule

8:30 A.M.— 9:00 A.M.	Bus arrives. Children are greeted as they come off the bus. Go into classroom for "free play."
9:00 A.M.— 9:15 A.M.	Morning greeting and songs. Work with mirror, counting of children.
9:15 A.M.— 9:30 A.M.	Some children in standing table, others grouped around the table. Work with rhythm instruments. Work with object identification.
9:30 A.M.—10:00 A.M.	Exercises, maze activity.
10:00 A.M.—11:00 A.M.	Work period (geared to child's level of development, pre-academic).
11:00 A.M.—11:30 A.M.	Outdoor activity when possible; otherwise, indoor games.
11:30 A.M.—11:45 A.M.	Preparation for lunch.
11:45 A.M.—12:30 P.M.	Lunch.

12:30 P.M.— 1:00 P.M.	Rest period.
1:00 P.M.— 1:45 P.M.	Art activities, rhythm dances.
1:45 P.M.— 2:00 P.M.	Preparation for going home.
2:00 P.M.	Teacher takes children outdoors to wait for the bus.

This schedule also provides time for individual work. During the 9:30 to 10:00 A.M. period, individual children may work with a physical therapist. All periods are kept fairly short to make allowance for a child's short interest span.

The emphasis in devising any schedule should be on creating an effective framework. It must give the day a structured format, whereby activities take place in sequence. Within that structure the teacher makes allowances for individual needs. The structure is a basis, and no teacher should run her class merely to keep up with a schedule. The example given above has been used successfully with a beginning group of multiply handicapped young children.

Bibliography

Barbe, Walter B. *The Exceptional Child.* Center for Applied Research, University of Illinois, 1963.

Benda, C.E. *Developmental Disorders of Mentation and Cerebral Palsies.* New York: Grune & Stratton, 1952.

Bender, Lauretta. *Psychopathology of Children with Organic Brain Disorders.* Springfield, Ill.: Charles C. Thomas, 1956.

Bettelheim, Bruno. *Love Is Not Enough.* Glencoe, Ill.: Free Press, 1950.

Bruner, Jerome S. "Going Beyond the Information." In *Contemporary Approaches to Cognition.* Cambridge, Mass.: Harvard University Press, 1957.

Carlson, Bernice, and Ginglend, D.R. *Play Activities for the Retarded Child.* Nashville, Tenn.: Abingdon Press, 1961.

Chukovsky, Kornie. *From Two to Five.* Berkeley, Calif.: University of California Press, 1963.

Connor, Francis P., and Talbot, Mable E. *An Experimental Curriculum for Young Mentally Retarded Children.* New York: Teachers College Press, Columbia University, 1964.

Cruickshank, William, and Johnson, Orville. *Education of Exceptional Children and Youth.* Englewood Cliffs, N.J.: Prentice-Hall, 1958.

Cutsforth, Thomas D. *The Blind in School and Society.* New York: American Foundation for the Blind, 1951.

Davens, Edward, "A View of Health Services for Mothers and Children." *Children* 12 (March-April 1965): 47-54.

Decker, Joan R. "Creative Art Experience for Blind Children." *The International Journal for the Education of the Blind,* May 1960, pp. 104-106.

Deutsch, Martin. "Facilitating Development in the Pre-School Child." In *Papers from the Arden House Conference on Pre-School Enrichment, Merrill-Palmer Quarterly of Behavior and Development* 10, no. 3 (1964): 249-263.

Diderot, Denis. *A Letter to a Person of Distinction.* Literature on the Blind, vol. 1, 1773 (Reprint). London: Sampson, Low, Marston, & Co., 1885.

Eaton, Allen K. *Beauty for the Sighted and the Blind.* New York: St. Martin's Press, 1959.

Ellis, Richard R. *The Facilitation of Learning for Environmentally Impoverished Children: Implications from Research Institute for Developmental Studies.* New York: Department of Psychiatry, New York Medical College, May 1964.

Erickson, Marion J. *The Mentally Retarded Child in the Classroom.* New York: Macmillan Co., 1965.

"Focus on Children and Youth." In *White House Conference on Children and Youth.* 50th ed. Washington, D.C., 1960.

Fraiberg, Selma H. *The Magic Years.* New York: Scribner's, 1959.

Frampton, Merle E.; Kenney, Ellen; and Schattner, Regina. *Forgotten Children.* Boston, Mass.: F. Porter Sargent, 1969.

Goldberg, I. Ignacy. *Selected Bibliography of Special Education.* New York: Teachers College Press, Columbia University, 1968.

Haring, Norris G.; Stern, George G.; and Cruickshank, William M. *Attitudes of Educators Toward Exceptional Children.* Syracuse, N.Y.: Syracuse University Press, 1958.

————, and Phillips, E. Larkin. *Educating Emotionally Disturbed Children.* New York: McGraw-Hill Book Co., 1962.

Hymes, James L. "Early Childhood." *Children* 7 (May-June 1960): 111-113.

Ingram, C.P. *Education of the Slow-Learning Child.* New York: The Ronald Press, 1960.

Johnson, Wendell. *Speech Handicapped School Children,* 3rd edition. New York: Harper & Row, 1967.

Josselyn, Irena M., *The Happy Child.* New York: Random House, 1955.

Langer, Susanne K. *Philosophy in a New Key.* New York: The New American Library, 1951.

Langdon, Grace. *Your Child's Play.* Chicago: National Society for Crippled Children and Adults, 1957.

Lemkau, Paul V. "The Influence of Handicapping Conditions on Child Development." *Children* 8 (March-April 1961): 43-47.

Lennox, William G. *Science and Seizures.* New York: Harper & Bros., 1946.

Lewis, R.S.; Strauss, Alfred A.; and Lehtinen, Laura E. *The Other Child.* New York: Grune & Stratton, 1951.

Long, Wilma J. "An Exploratory Study of the Use of Role Playing with Severely Retarded Children." *American Journal of Mental Deficiency* 63 (1959):784-791.

Lowenfeld, Berthold. *Our Blind Children.* Springfield, Ill.: Charles C. Thomas, 1964.

Lowenfeld, Viktor. *Creative and Mental Growth.* New York: Macmillan Co., 1957.

Luria, Alexandre R., *The Nature of Human Conflicts.* Translated and edited by W. Horsley Gant. New York: Grove Press, 1960.

————. *The Role of Speech in the Regulation of Normal and Abnormal Behavior.* New York: Liveright, 1961.

————. *Speech and Development of Mental Processes in the Child.* London: Staples Press, 1959.

Mackintosh, Helen K., ed. 1964. *Children and Oral Language* (Statement by a Joint Committee of the ACEI, ASCE, IRA, and NCTE). U.S. Office of Education.

Magary, J.D., and Eichorn, J.R. *The Exceptional Child.* New York: Holt, Rinehart and Winston, 1961.

Marland, Sidney P., Jr. "Ferment in the Schools." *Children* 12 (March-April 1965): 62-68.

Mathews, Donald K.; Kruse, Robert; and Shaw, Virginia. *The Science of Physical Education for Handicapped Children.* New York: Harper & Bros., 1962.

Mead, Margaret. 1962. *A Creative Life for Your Children.* U.S. Department of Health, Education and Welfare, Children's Bureau.

Menninger, Karl. *Psychiatric Aspects of Physical Disability.* Office of Vocational Rehabilitation (HEW) Publication 210. Washington D.C., 1952.

Menolascino, Frank J. "Emotional Disturbance and Mental Retardation." *American Journal of Mental Deficiency* 70 (1965):-248-256.

Norris, Miriam; Spaulding, Patricia J.; and Brodie, Fern H. *Blindness in Children.* Chicago: University of Chicago Press, 1957.

Oettinger, Katherine B. "Looking Back and Ahead." *Children* 12 (March-April 1965):43-46.

Phelps, Winthrop. *The Cerebral Palsied Child: A Guide for Parents.* New York: Simon & Schuster, 1958.

Piaget, Jean. *The Language and Thought of the Child.* New York: Meridian Books, 1960.

———. *Play, Dreams and Imitation in Childhood.* New York: Norton, 1962.

Pomeroy, Janet. *Recreation for the Physically Handicapped.* New York: Macmillan Co., 1964.

Radaker, Leon D. "The Visual Imagery of Retarded Children." *Exceptional Children* 27 (1961):524-531.

Robins, Ferris, and Robins, Jennet. *Educational Rhythmics for Mentally Handicapped Children: A Method of Practical Application.* New York: Horizon Press Publishers, 1965.

Roderick, Martha M. "Exceptional Children Develop Through Art Expression." *New Outlook for the Blind,* April 1956, pp. 2-7.

Schattner, Regina. *Creative Dramatics for Handicapped Children.* New York: John Day Co., 1967.

Strauss, Alfred A., and Lehtinen, Laura E. *Psychopathology and Education of the Brain Injured Child,* vol. 1. New York: Grune & Stratton, 1947.

————, and Kephart, Newell C. *Psychopathology and Education of the Brain Injured Child,* vol. 2. New York: Grune & Stratton, 1955.

Taylor, E.M. *Psychological Appraisal of Children with Cerebral Defects.* Cambridge, Mass.: Harvard University Press, 1959.

Taylor, Harris, and Olsen, K. "Team Teaching with Trainable Mentally Retarded Children." *Exceptional Children* 30 (1964):-304-309.

Thayer, Eleanor W. "Music, Kindergarten Through the Elementary Grades." American Association of Instructors of the Blind, 1950.

Toomer, Joan M., and Brown, S. Colborne. "Learning Through Play." *The New Beacon,* 48 (1964):409–412; 437–440.

United Cerebral Palsy Associations. *Realistic Educational Planning for Children with Cerebral Palsy—Pre-Elementary School Level,* Pamphlet #2. New York, 1952.

Vygotsky, L. *Thought and Language.* Edited and translated by E. Haufman and G. Vakar. New York: Wiley, 1962.

Whatmough, Joshua. *Language.* New York: The New American Library, 1957.

White House Conference on Children and Youth. 50th ed. Conference Proceedings. Washington, D.C., 1960.

Zahl, Paul. *Blindness.* New York: Hafner Publishing Co., 1962.